G⊙D

for the 21st Century

Edited by Russell Stannard

TEMPLETON FOUNDATION PRESS : PHILADELPHIA

TEMPLETON FOUNDATION PRESS

Five Radnor Corporate Center, Suite 120

Radnor, Pennsylvania 19087

© 2000 by Templeton Foundation Press

Printed in the United States of America

Library of Congress Cataloging-in-Publication Data

God for the 21st century / edited by Russell Stannard

p. cm.   ISBN 1-890151-36-x (alkaline paper)

I. Religion and science.   II. Title: God for the twenty-
first century.   III. Stannard, Russell

BL240.2.G62 2000   215–dc21   99-048054

Published in Great Britain in 2000 by

SPCK, Holy Trinity Church, Marylebone Road, London NW1 4DU

British Library Cataloguing-in-Publication Data

A catalogue record for this book is available from the British Library.

ISBN 0-281-053-42-1

00 01 02 03 04 05 06 10   9 8 7 6 5 4 3 2 1

Contents

Preface

RUSSELL STANNARD

Modern science has revolutionized our understanding of the world. This much is obvious. But how have these developments impacted on our knowledge of God? And how do we now see human beings fitting into the overall scheme?

To find out, I approached fifty leading figures noted for their contributions to the ongoing discussion of the interrelationships between science and religion. I asked each to write a short essay on some aspect of the way our thinking should be revised in the light of what is known at the dawn of the twenty-first century. The contributions were not to be scholarly treatises aimed at fellow academics, but informal writings accessible to a wide readership. Many of the essays produced have subsequently appeared in newspapers and magazines worldwide—elegant testimony to how well the authors succeeded in this regard.

The writers are drawn from eight countries and represent the Christian, Jewish, Islamic, and Hindu traditions. Most are scientists by profession, but also included are philosophers, theologians, and psychologists. The topics range from cosmology, evolution, and genetic engineering to extraterrestrial life, the soul, and the current status of the science/religion debate. Taken together, the authors present a challenging and enriched understanding of God and of God's interaction with the world and with ourselves.

ACKNOWLEDGMENTS

The editor and contributors wish to thank the John Templeton Foundation for its support in making this volume possible.

Special thanks are due to Gregg Easterbrook for his advice and constant help throughout the project.

ix

Part One

Origins

We begin at the beginning: how the universe came into being. Initially, everything was squashed together at a point. There was a Big Bang; the universe expanded and has continued doing so ever since.

Much has been written on the topic in recent times, including books aimed at the mass market. Given the nature of the subject, it is perhaps not surprising that the authors of these books sometimes find themselves straying beyond the confines of their science to venture a few thoughts on how the new findings affect traditional ideas about a Creator God. Such digressions often lead to conclusions that appear damaging to belief in God. Are they justified?

For a start, there is the claim that the modern scientific view renders worthless the biblical account of creation. That would be so if the Genesis account were intended as a literal description of our origins—which seems most unlikely. **Ted Burge's** modernized creation story gets across the same divine truth that the world and we are ultimately dependent for our existence on God, but does so in a way that accords with our modern understanding of cosmology.

Rod Davies, formerly in charge of the famous Jodrell Bank radio telescope, sees his probings into the mysteries of the early universe as not only a scientific exploration but also an awesome religious quest.

Paul Davies points out that the Big Bang was no ordinary explosion; it did not occur at a point in time. Rather, it marked the *beginning* of time. As St. Augustine deduced some 1,500 years ago, time is a feature, or property, of the world, and as such needed to be created along with everything else. Many people are disturbed to learn that there could have been no God before the Big Bang—because there was no "before." Davies clarifies what it means to think of God as "Creator."

A Creation Story for Our Times

TED BURGE

The Big Bang and subsequent physical and biological evolution are firmly established beliefs in the minds of nearly all scientists. When set side by side with the story of creation in Genesis, they appear to give a more convincing account of the material creation. But the two accounts have different purposes. The scientific one, of course, makes no mention of God. Genesis, on the other hand, is primarily concerned with the divine truths of God and creation and God's relation to humankind.

Those parts of Genesis that reveal primitive ideas about the material aspects of creation can be revised without disturbing most of those divine truths. We have much evidence in the Bible of the evolution of the concept of God, particularly in the Old Testament, but belief in him as Creator and our dependence on him remain firm and unchanged.

In the light of our present scientific knowledge and of subsequent events in history, perhaps the writers of Genesis, inspired by God's continuing revelation of himself, would have written something like this: In the beginning, God said "Let there be . . . ," and he created the unified forces of physics, with perfect symmetry and prescient precision. And out of nothing, and into nothing, God, by a free decision, set up the spontaneous production of particles, in newborn space and time, producing a silent, seething sphere, infinitesimally small and unimaginably hot. There was onset and evolution, the first stage of creation.

During a tiny fraction of a second, an expansion took place, and the perfect symmetry of the forces was broken, step by step, as the temperature dropped, to produce the forces of nature we know today.

God's well-tuned laws made innumerable particles, of every requisite kind, in a steadily expanding chaotic cooling sphere. And the universe cooled for nearly a million years, until electrons could stay joined to nuclei to form familiar atoms. There was onset and evolution, the second stage of creation.

With atoms and molecules as building blocks, the attracting force of gravity took over, and after about a thousand million years, God saw the first stars and galaxies forming in an expanding cosmic universe. There was onset and evolution, the third stage of creation.

Individual stars contracted under gravity and became hot enough for nuclear fusion to produce chemical elements not seen before, until, after about ten thousand million years, stars were exhausted by their radiance, and God saw them begin to die, some dramatically, by exploding as supernovas, releasing all the known chemical elements. There was onset and evolution, the fourth stage of creation.

And God saw that it was very good, for now all the ingredients were available, and gravity formed a second generation of stars, some accompanied by planets and satellites, including the Sun, Earth, and, later, the Moon, in our galaxy of the Milky Way. There was onset and evolution, the fifth stage of creation.

Bathed in alternate daylight and darkness, during the next thousand million years or so, conditions on Earth became favorable for the eventual generation of life. There was onset and evolution, the sixth stage of creation.

During these last three thousand million years, life has evolved as God intended, and through numerous cycles of birth, survival, procreation, and death, species have multiplied and progressed, plants and animals of every kind, and some have become extinct, until, a mere three hundred thousand years ago, there arrived, in the likeness of God, *Homo sapiens*, intelligent humans, with freedom to choose, living together in community, knowing good and evil, pleasure and pain, aware of honor due to their dominion, and acquainted with death. There was onset and evolution, the seventh stage of creation.

And the universe entered the Age of Humanity. Human beings have hardly changed in physical form during the past forty thousand years, but their beliefs have evolved, their knowledge has grown, and their understanding has deepened.

And God saw that it was good, but it was not good enough, for free will led to sin and suffering, and guilt and disbelief could lead to despair and the death of the human spirit.

So God sent his only Son, the Word made flesh, who dwelt among us as Jesus of Nazareth, suffered, died, and rose from the dead, and showed his glory, full of grace and truth.

And that was the beginning of the new creation.

•

Ted Burge is Emeritus Professor of Physics of the University of London and former Dean of the Faculty of Science. He also holds a degree in theology. Burge is the author of Atomic Nuclei and Their Particles, Lord of All, Hear Our Prayer, *and* Lord for All Seasons.

The Alpha and the Omega of Space and Time

ROD DAVIES

The study of the origins of the universe is, I believe, both a scientific and a religious voyage of discovery: scientific because we use the techniques of the scientific method—exploration and deduction; religious because it contains the element of awe and wonder, and it stimulates questions about purpose and ends.

The current scientific view is that the cosmos began with a Big Bang. The universe is expanding from a compact phase of condensed matter at the beginning of time.

As we examine the more distant galaxies, we are probing further back in time as a consequence of the finite speed of light. When I first came into astronomy in early 1950, the light from the most distant galaxies then detected had been traveling for a billion years—one-fifteenth of the age of the universe. Radio astronomy today can take us closer to the Big Bang: to within three hundred thousand years.

This arises out of observations of the cosmic microwave back-ground—the "afterglow" of the Big Bang itself. This form of radiation is extremely uniformly distributed across the whole sky. But in the past twenty years slight inhomogeneities have been detected. Encoded in these variations are the earliest clues we have so far detected as to how the universe came to acquire the structure it has today. It was these slight variations of density and temperature that were subsequenly to be re-inforced by the influence of gravity, giving rise to the galaxies we see today. From within these spinning galaxies, the stars, the planets, and eventually we ourselves emerged. Much of my recent scientific effort has been devoted to the search for these weak and elusive signals—clues to the secrets of the origin of the universe.

It is possible to get even closer to the instant of the Big Bang using a different kind of observation. Although the element helium is produced in stars through the fusion of hydrogen, it was also present before the earliest stars formed. The only environment with sufficiently high energies capable of such cosmic alchemy was the first few hundred *seconds* of the history of the universe. The study of the primordial abundances of the elements becomes another way of exploring the conditions of the early universe.

One of the most important outstanding problems is the determination of the average mass density of the universe. If we could find its precise value, we could determine the ultimate fate of the cosmos.

If the density of the universe is high enough, the gravitational pull of each part on every other part will eventually bring the expansion to a halt and, billions of years into the future, cause everything to collapse in on itself in a Big Crunch.

On the other hand, if the density is too low, the universe will expand forever, becoming more and more tenuous, with the galaxies receding farther and farther from each other.

A third intriguing possibility is suggested by a theory called the "inflationary scenario." This holds that a tiny fraction of a second after the instant of the Big Bang, there was a change of state of the radiation/matter mix, resulting in a density that will eventually lead to the expansion approaching a gradual halt—in the infinite future.

So much for a sketchy summary of the present scientific thinking about the origins and ultimate destiny of the universe. What then about my opening statement that the quest for the origin of the universe is a journey of discovery for both scientific and religious thinkers?

The Judeo-Christian reaching out for an understanding of our origins is encapsulated in Genesis:

"In the beginning God created the heaven and the Earth. And the

Earth was without form, and void; and darkness was on the face of the deep. And the spirit of God moved on the face of the waters. And God said, 'Let there be light'; and there was light."

In the New Testament we have the Greek philosophical addition. John sums it up beautifully in his Gospel:

"In the beginning was the Word, and the Word was with God, and the Word was God. The same was in the beginning with God. All things were made by Him; and without Him was not anything made that was made. In Him was life; and the life was the light of men. And the light shineth in the darkness; and the darkness comprehended it not. . . . He was in the world, and the world was made by Him."

In this concept of the "Word," or *logos*, we have the kernel of what the Christian believes about God the Creator. Having created the world, God is in the world and part of it. In him we have our being. If we get our minds "around" this philosophical concept, the scientific approach to creation and the religious approach merge.

Today we too attempt to make sense of the world and the communities in which we live in response to wonder and reverence for the created order. The scientists ask how it is that all the processes which have operated over the billions of years since the Big Bang led to the emergence of a *Homo sapiens* who can contemplate the whole creative process. This is summed up in the anthropic principle, which affirms that the universe must have within it those properties which allow life to develop at some stage of its history. "The most unintelligible thing about the universe is that it is intelligible," said Albert Einstein. In such recent thinking, I begin to see a synthesis of the scientific and religious approaches to the wonder and potential of creation.

•

Rod Davies is Emeritus Professor of Radio Astronomy at the University of Manchester and former director of the Nuffield Radio Astronomy Laboratories, Jodrell Bank. He is also a Methodist preacher.

What Happened before the Big Bang?

PAUL DAVIES

It is often said that science cannot prove the existence of God. Yet science does have value in theological debate because it gives us new concepts that sometimes make popular notions of God untenable. One of these concerns the nature of time.

Many people envisage God as a sort of cosmic magician who existed for all eternity, and then at some moment in the past created the universe in a gigantic supernatural act. Unfortunately, this scenario raises some awkward questions. What was God doing before he created the universe? If God is a perfect, unchanging being, what prompted him to act then rather than sooner? The fifth-century theologian St. Augustine neatly solved the problem by proclaiming that the world was made *with* time and not *in* time. In other words, time itself is part of God's creation.

To make sense of Augustine's concept it is necessary to place God outside of time altogether, and the notion of a timeless Deity became official church doctrine. However, it is not without its own difficulties. How can a timeless God be involved with temporal events in the universe, such as entering into human history through the Incarnation?

Today, religious people like to identify the creation with the Big Bang of scientific cosmology. So what can we say about the nature of time in the scientific picture?

Albert Einstein showed us that time and space are part of the physical world, just as much as matter and energy. Indeed, time can be manipulated in the laboratory. Dramatic time warps occur, for example, when subatomic particles are accelerated to near the speed of light. Black holes stretch time by an infinite amount. It is therefore wrong to think of time as simply "there," as a universal, eternal backdrop to existence. So a complete theory of the universe needs to explain not only how matter and energy came to exist; it must explain the origin of time, too.

Happily, Einstein's theory of relativity is up to the job. It predicts a so-called singularity at which time abruptly starts. In the standard Big Bang scenario, time and space come into being spontaneously at such a singularity, along with matter.

People often ask, What happened before the Big Bang? The answer is, Nothing. By this, I do not mean that there was a state of nothingness, pregnant with creative power. There was nothing before the Big Bang because there was no such epoch as "before." As Stephen Hawking has remarked, asking what happened before the Big Bang is rather like asking what lies north of the North Pole. The answer, once again, is nothing, not because there exists a mysterious Land of Nothing there, but because there is no such place as north of the North Pole. Similarly, there is no such time as "before the Big Bang." Of course, one can still ask why a universe popped into existence this way. Cosmologists believe the answer lies with the weird properties of quantum mechanics, a topic beyond the scope of this essay.

We can now see that Augustine was right and popular religion wrong to envisage God as a superbeing dwelling within the stream of time prior to the creation. Professional theologians acknowledge this. The doctrine of creation ex nihilo (out of nothing) does not mean God pushing a metaphysical button and making a Big Bang, then sitting back to watch the action. It means God sustaining the existence of the universe, and its laws, at all times, from a location outside of space and time.

Can science give any credibility to such a notion? Mostly, scientists either are atheists or keep God in a separate mental compartment. However, there is a strong parallel in the scientific concept of the laws of nature. Like the theologians' God, these laws enjoy an abstract, timeless existence, and are capable of bringing the universe into being from nothing. But where do they come from? And why do these laws exist rather than some different set?

Science is based on the assumption that the universe is thoroughly rational and logical at all levels. Miracles are not allowed. This implies that there should be reasons for the particular laws of nature that regulate the physical universe. Atheists claim that the laws exist reasonlessly and that the universe is ultimately absurd. As a scientist, I find this hard to accept. There must be an unchanging rational ground in which the logical, orderly nature of the universe is rooted. Is this rational ground like the timeless God of Augustine? Perhaps it is. But in any case, the lawlike basis of the universe seems a more fruitful place for a dialogue between science and theology than focusing on the origin of the universe and the discredited notion of what happened before the Big Bang.

•

Paul Davies is Visiting Professor of Physics at Imperial College in London. Formerly he was Professor of Theoretical Physics at the University of Newcastle and Professor of Mathematical Physics and of Natural Philosophy at the University of Adelaide, Australia. Davies was awarded the 1995 Templeton Prize for Progress in Religion and is the author of more than twenty best-selling books, most notably The Mind of God.

Part Two

The Universe as a Home for Life

At first sight the universe appears to be a vast and hostile place—hardly a suitable "home" for life. But looks are deceptive. For intelligent life to evolve from what was originally a fireball, the world had to satisfy a range of conditions—collectively known as the *anthropic principle*.

Michael Poole and **Owen Gingerich** point out that the universe had to have the characteristics it possesses in order for us to put in an appearance. This fine-tuning does not in itself constitute a knockdown proof of a Designer God, but it is, nevertheless, fully consistent with there being a purpose behind creation.

Bruno Guiderdoni, in contemplating the cooled-down remnant of the primordial fireball, notes that although it is almost uniform in its distribution, close examination reveals a pattern of gentle irregularities. It was these inhomogeneities that were later to develop into life-bearing galaxies. He regards this radiation map as an icon for our times—the might of God and the subtlety of humankind combined into a single image.

Howard Van Till emphasizes that there is deep mystery in the way the ultimate constituents of the world, and the laws that govern their behavior, have the ability to transform the simple raw materials and energy emerging from the Big Bang into the intricate forms that constitute us and our surroundings. This gift of self-organization, so easily taken for granted, is perhaps best seen as evidence of a creative Mind.

Of course, not everyone agrees that the study of the world leads inevitably to contemplation of God. **Carl Feit** points out from a Jewish perspective that in a complex way God reveals himself in nature but also remains hidden.

Finally, **Gregg Easterbrook** traces how the once pervasive view that the universe is "pointless," and life "a cosmic joke," is steadily giving way to a more buoyant and meaningful assessment of humanity.

Big and Old and Dark and Cold

MICHAEL POOLE

Is our universe user-friendly? Not obviously, for it is big and old and dark and cold. So it is easy for anyone who stares up into the night sky to feel insignificant. After all we are about six feet tall in a universe which is seventy thousand billion, billion miles across. We only last seventy years; the universe has been around for twelve thousand million of them.

Several millennia ago, when that Hebrew shepherd boy, David, later to become king, gazed up into the night sky he certainly thought that he was significant. He later talked about being made "a little lower than the heavenly beings." But whereas David could have counted no more than a thousand stars while he guarded his sheep against night prowlers, telescopes show that our own galaxy—the Milky Way—contains some hundred thousand million stars. And there are another hundred thousand million galaxies. That amounts to two million, million stars for every man, woman, and child alive today! How about significance in that sort of a world?

One reading of these large numbers reinforces feelings of human insignificance. But an alternative offers a new twist, one which goes like this:

It takes billions of years for the building blocks of life to be formed in stars, so, for us to be here, the universe has to be very old.

As a result of the Big Bang, matter moved off at nearly 186,000 miles a second—the speed of light. Keep traveling at that kind of speed for twelve billion years and you will go far! So the universe has not only to be old but also big.

The Big Bang was violent and it was hot. But because an expanding universe gets cold, and this expansion has been going on for a very long time, the universe is now colder than anything to be found on Earth outside the specialized conditions set up in low-temperature laboratories.

So we should not be surprised to find the universe the way it is.

As regards the development of the universe following the Big Bang, much depends on the density of matter. It is the gravitational attraction between matter that tends to slow down the expansion. Professor Stephen Hawking has suggested that "if the density of the universe one second after the Big Bang had been greater by one part in a thousand billion, the universe would have recollapsed after ten years. On the other hand, if the density of the universe at that time had been less by the same amount, the universe would have been essentially empty since it was about ten years old."

Professor Paul Davies has discussed how precise the matching of the outward exploding thrust of the Big Bang and the inward gravitational attraction needed to be in the early universe for life subsequently to develop. He points out that "the matching was accurate to a staggering one part in 10^{60}. That is to say, had the explosion differed in strength at the outset by only one part in 10^{60}, the universe we now perceive would not exist. To give some meaning to these numbers, suppose you wanted to fire a bullet at a one-inch target on the other side of the observable universe, twenty billion light years away. Your aim would have to be accurate to that same part in 10^{60}."

That was but one of many "coincidences" that had to be satisfied for life to put in an appearance. The physical constants governing the strength of the forces and other characteristics of nature also had to be finely poised for us to be here. Take, for example, gravity:

Out of the Big Bang there came mostly the lightest gases, hydrogen and helium. These needed to be fused together to cook up the heavier elements like carbon, nitrogen, and oxygen, which are the building blocks of life. The high-temperature, high-pressure conditions found in the interior of stars provide the ovens for doing this. Some stars then blow up when they are old, scattering these heavier elements into space, eventually making up our bodies.

But how do stars form in the first place? Through gravity compressing a cloud of gas, heating it in the process, and igniting the nuclear fusion fires. Make gravity any weaker, and the stars will not ignite. Make it any stronger, and the stars will be so massive they will burn too fast and long-lived stars like the Sun will not exist.

Do these and other coincidences amount to a knockdown argument for the existence of a Designer God? I don't think so. Knockdown arguments for God are always suspect, perhaps because many believers don't see God as forcing people into corners from which there is no escape. What can be said is that this view of the universe is entirely consistent with belief in God. There is nothing irrational in believing in a Creator who made the universe with us in mind. Certainly there are scientific answers to why the universe developed the way it did, but they still leave unanswered the question of why there is a universe at all with the properties which gave rise to us.

If such speculations do point in any way toward a purposeful God, they point little further than to some remote originator of the universe. The turn of the millennium, however, directs our attention to history rather than to science for answers about purpose. It commemorates, and for many people celebrates, someone who claimed to be God incarnate —incarnate with a body made up of the ashes of long-dead stars. As if that claim was not staggering enough, he claimed to die for our sins, to defeat death by rising from the dead, and to be able and willing to show us the purpose for our lives today.

•

Michael Poole is Visiting Research Fellow at the School of Education, King's College, London. He is the author of Guide to Science and Belief.

17

Ingredients for Life

OWEN GINGERICH

Fourteen billion years ago—give or take a billion—the entire universe exploded into existence. But it was a lifeless universe, lacking the two most vital ingredients for life: water and carbon.

Over the next billions of years the universe was gradually transformed into a most congenial home for intelligent life. The missing elements were forged in giant cauldrons deep within evolving stars. Was this an unlikely accident? Or the consequence of incredible design? When you look at the details, it is hard to escape the conclusion, propounded by astrophysicist Sir Fred Hoyle, that a superintelligence was at work.

In the opening minutes of the Big Bang, the cataclysmic explosion that started off our universe produced the two simplest elements, hydrogen and helium. These atoms were formed in huge abundance. But the universe expanded too fast for nuclear collisions to create heavier elements such as carbon and oxygen.

Without oxygen there would be no water, and without carbon no organic chemistry. Without these essential atoms, there would be no you or I. So, where did they come from?

A century ago there was no answer to this question. If you had asked a physicist, he probably would have told you to get lost. In the past fifty years, the answer has been found: giant stars did it.

Most stars shine by hydrogen fusion, using nuclear reactions to change hydrogen into helium. (This is the same energy source exploited by hydrogen bombs.) When the hydrogen fuel inside the core of a giant star is exhausted, the star's core begins to collapse, raising the millions-of-degrees temperature still higher until the helium itself catches on fire. Well, not exactly fire in the terrestrial sense, but a kind of nuclear bonfire where helium atoms smash into each other with such violence that three of them can stick together to form carbon. The more massive stars eventually become supernovas, blowing themselves up and scattering the newly formed atoms into space, where they eventually coalesce to form new stars and planets.

Triple collisions are so rare inside stars that the carbon-forming process wouldn't amount to much, except for what physicists call a resonance level, an energy state inside the carbon nucleus that helps the process along. Back in 1953, the young astrophysicist Fred Hoyle predicted the existence of such a resonance, and the nuclear physicist Willy Fowler, to his astonishment, found the level experimentally very close to where Hoyle had predicted it. Had this level been 4 percent lower, there would simply not be enough carbon for organic life on Earth. Had the similar resonance level in oxygen been only half a percent higher, almost all of the carbon would have been turned into oxygen. Either way, we wouldn't be here.

Is the nuclear structure of the oxygen and carbon atoms just a lucky coincidence? Or is it evidence of intelligent design? Fred Hoyle was so impressed by this discovery that he wrote: "Would you not say to yourself, 'Some supercalculating intellect must have designed the properties of the carbon atom, otherwise the chance of my finding such an atom through the blind forces of nature would be utterly minuscule?' Of course you would. . . . A commonsense interpretation of the facts suggests that a superintellect has monkeyed with physics. . . . The numbers one calculates from the facts seem to me so overwhelming as to put this conclusion almost beyond question."

By now scientists have found an impressive array of such "coincidences." Without these many details of the physical and chemical world, intelligent life wouldn't exist in our universe. Scientists have given this observation a name: the anthropic principle. The basic idea is that the universe simply must be this way, as otherwise we wouldn't be alive to observe it.

Needless to say, for several decades theists and atheists have been wrangling over the meaning of the anthropic principle. For the theists, the anthropic principle may not be a proof of God's existence, but it is surely a pointer to a creative superintelligence at work. They would go along with Walt Whitman, who, when answering the question, "What is grass?" wrote, "I guess it is the handkerchief of the Lord, a scented gift and remembrancer designedly dropt."

Some cosmologists have recently turned up an intriguing counter-argument. The Big Bang explosion may have spawned a vast number of sister universes, with entirely different physical circumstances. Some would have expanded too rapidly for stars and galaxies to form. Others might have very different physical laws, even a different number of di-mensions. In the vast majority, life would be impossible or unlikely. In the "multiuniverse" model, we would find ourselves in the rare universe that is suitable for life. Instead of a universe specifically designed for our existence, we would necessarily be in the one that was accidentally right for intelligent life. And that, say the atheists, is that.

The theists point out that any other such universes would be forever invisible. We could only accept them on faith because there would be no possible way to observe them. So, say the theists, everyone must accept something on faith, and it's an interesting choice to make.

For some astronomers, the multiuniverse picture of the cosmos is a consequence of the fluctuations in the light from the most distant parts of the observable universe, and they see no theological implications at all in the idea. Some cosmologists are personally theists, some are atheists. But they are universally awed by the sweep and grandeur of the cosmos.

•

Owen Gingerich is Senior Astronomer at the Smithsonian Astrophysical Observatory and Professor of Astronomy and the History of Science at Harvard University; formerly he was vice president of the American Philosophical Society. Among his four hundred publications is Album of Science: The Physical Sciences in the Twentieth Century.

An Icon for the Millennium

BRUNO GUIDERDONI

The cosmos appears vast, dark, and hostile to life. Much of the universe is indeed inhospitable. But the study of space can also present us with images of a very different sort—images that can profoundly affect our thinking in positive ways.

On Christmas Eve 1968, astronauts Frank Borman, Jim Lovell, and William Anders aboard *Apollo 8* were struck by the beauty and frailty of our planet. They were in the first inhabited flight orbiting the Moon. Through the window of their narrow spacecraft, the Earth appeared as a round blue fruit lost in the vastness of space. What a contrast with the dead surface of the Moon! While reading the first verses of Genesis, they became suddenly aware that, from such a distance, the differences between nations vanished. As a consequence, we urgently had to learn how to live together peacefully. The pictures of the Earth they brought back from their heavenly journey gave a strong impression: a new environmental awareness and sense of responsibility for all humankind. Though I was only ten years old at that time, I still remember my fascination when I contemplated our fragile harbor surrounded by darkness.

Since then, we have learned a lot about the cosmos. In particular, it has come to be recognized that, in a deep and subtle sense, the cosmos is not at all hostile to life. Our existence was made possible only by the occurrence of many coincidences.

For example, matter is ruled by a subtle balance between the laws of nature that made stars able to form in gas clouds and to gently cook heavy elements, such as carbon, nitrogen, and oxygen—elements essential for the later development of life.

The initial Big Bang gave the right beginning to the expansion of the universe so that we could live in it later. Had the thrust at the beginning been stronger, cosmic matter would have been quickly diluted. No galaxy would have formed, which means no stars, no planets, no life. Had it been weaker, cosmic matter would have slowed expansion down so quickly that the universe would have recollapsed too early to let stars make heavy elements.

In the 1980s, several physicists proposed a mechanism for the Big Bang. They stated that the initial thrust of the Bang, some twelve billion years ago, arose out of a process called "cosmic inflation." Space inflated by more than thirty orders of magnitude in an incredibly small amount of time—a minuscule fraction of a second. This brief period of superfast expansion stretched tiny fluctuations in the initial distribution of matter and transformed them into large-scale irregularities. These were the seeds from which the galaxies were later to form through the operation of gravity.

Well, that sounds like speculation, doesn't it? How can one possibly know what happened so long ago? But no, this is not guesswork; this is science. The theory sticks its neck out to be tested. And it will be tested, in the beginning of this new millennium. Because it takes time for light to reach us from a distance, the farther away we look, the farther back in time we look. God has apparently chosen to let us know some of the secrets of the origins, through light coming from far away and long ago.

What we find is that the light initially emitted at the Big Bang can still be detected today. Since that time it has cooled down so that it is now observable as microwave radiation. Arno Penzias and Robert Wilson discovered this relict radiation in 1965. This is the most ancient radiation in the universe. It originates from the farthest surface of all that we can actually see. It was expected that the seeds of the galaxies would have left an imprint on this cosmic radiation: slightly warmer or colder areas on the sky. The temperature differences are small, about one part in one hundred thousand. But our detectors are now so sensitive that we can map them.

In 1989, the *Cosmic Background Explorer* was launched by NASA to check that the imprint was indeed there. We now know it is. However, if we want to test that inflation actually did take place in the very earliest stages of the development of the Bang, we need to look at these ripples in greater detail. In the fall of 2000, NASA will launch another satellite, the *Microwave Anisotropy Probe* (MAP), to observe the features of this radiation with one hundred times more resolution. This spacecraft will have to venture beyond the orbit of the Moon, to avoid its detectors being swamped by stray light coming from the Earth. It will settle in darkness, at one million miles from our blue planet. Over a period of two years, it will gaze at the relict radiation to make a map of the ripples. Then powerful computers will analyze the map and check whether our ideas on the origin of the Big Bang and galaxies are true.

In this map will be written the sheer power of the laws that have moved the universe. The same picture will also reveal the gentleness that has allowed structure to develop—the formation of the galaxies and, in due course, our own existence. The might of God and the subtlety of humankind will be gathered into a single image.

This makes me think of the icons featured in Eastern Christianity. They too radiate a light—a golden light that recalls both God's power in creation, and the human face. This new icon will be circulated in the first years of the millennium. It should be the sign of a novel alliance that should reconcile humanity with the cosmos.

By reflecting upon this illuminating image, we should remember that, even if the astronauts of *Apollo 8* reminded us that the Earth is lost in dark space, this darkness is not inhospitable. The vastness of space and time are necessary, as are the deserts of sand and ice that participate in the climatic balance of the Earth. In the most distant sky are kept the laws that provide us with this teaching. I look forward to contemplating this protective cosmic icon. A verse of the Koran springs to mind: "Our Lord, You embrace everything in Mercy and Knowledge."

•

Bruno Guiderdoni is a physicist at the Institut d'Astrophysique de Paris, where he studies the deep universe. He also writes, broadcasts, and lectures on Islamic doctrine and spirituality.

Why Does the Universe Work?

HOWARD VAN TILL

Can the "stuff" of the universe do everything that science expects of it? The world of whirling particles can do a lot, but does it have the abilities needed for transforming raw energy into atoms, and atoms into elephants, and us?

As scientists, we think it does. But, also as scientists, we haven't a clue as to why that should be the case. Why should the universe work well enough to make the processes of evolution possible? We have no scientific answer. Science is silent here.

Some people I know take this silence as evidence that divine intrusion was needed. The "God of special effects" often gets plugged in wherever there are gaps in today's scientific knowledge. Gaps in what we know are treated as if they were gaps in what the universe can do. Some people say, for instance, that God has had to intervene from time to time to start new forms of life.

But what if such interventions are not necessary? That would raise an even more interesting question, wouldn't it? How did the universe come to possess the abilities for organizing atoms into elephants? Science crafts clever theories about how things get formed, but why is the stuff of the universe able to arrange itself into these forms?

Why, for instance, should protons and neutrons be able to combine into the nuclei of a hundred different chemical elements? And why should the atoms of these elements be inclined to gather into molecules—from simple molecules like carbon dioxide to complex coils of DNA molecules essential for life? It would be so easy to imagine a universe with elementary constituents that did not have these gifts for forming things.

Questions of this sort are seldom asked in a typical science course. Having taught physics for many years, I know the usual routine. We tell students about the basic forces of interaction. We write down the "laws of physics" that provide us with a cause-and-effect story for what happens when things interact. That should settle it, right?

Perhaps. But it depends on what needs to be settled. If the question were simply, What happens when things interact? then the standard textbook approach would be adequate. But I want to ask a more profound question. I want to know why there are such things as interaction forces in the first place, and why things are gifted with the ability to respond to these forces in the particular ways that we observe.

In short, why does the universe work? Where do the universe's "natural" abilities come from? What is the ultimate source of the properties and interactions that we take for granted as ordinary? What we call "ordinary" turns out to be truly awesome when you think about it. I want to know where the universe gets its awesome character.

Science has no answers to questions like this. We scientists do a bang-up job of figuring out how things work. We've learned how to connect what happens to what abilities are being exercised. But when we ask why the universe should possess these particular abilities, we are forced to think about the ultimate Source of the universe's being. We must ask why there is something rather than nothing. And why is the something that exists (this universe) so well equipped with the abilities—the gifts —for organizing into new forms?

Ask a dozen people this question. See how differently they respond. Some will be content with glib appeals to chance or luck. Others will assert that the question has no answer and will suggest that you move on to more practical issues. Most would rather know the closing figures of the stock market.

But some of us still wonder at the giftedness of the universe. Is a facile appeal to happenstance enough? Or could it be that the universe is a creation? Could it be that the universe has been gifted by its Creator with all of the abilities needed to bring about new forms in time?

Suppose that the universe really is a creation. Then everything that the universe is and is able to do would have to be seen as a "gift of being" from the Creator. Furthermore, the more gifted the universe is, the more it owes to the creativity and generosity of the Creator. This sort of Creator cannot be confined to gaps carved by human ignorance.

There was a time when there were no living creatures of any sort on our planet. Oh, there may have been globs of biologically interesting molecules around, but they were not yet organized into living systems. But now there are lots of living things walking, swimming, crawling, and flying around. How did that astounding change come about?

If our scientific hunches are on the right track—and I do think they are—some of those interesting molecules had the abilities to self-organize into primitive forms of life. And those primitive organisms must also have had the gifts for diversifying into a vast array of novel forms in time.

Do these awesome gifts come spontaneously from nothing? I doubt it. Perhaps the awesome nature of the universe is best seen as evidence for a Mind more creative than we could imagine. Perhaps the giftedness of the universe is best seen as evidence for a Giver of Being more generous than we humans could ever envision.

•

Howard Van Till is Professor and Chairman of the Department of Physics at Calvin College in Grand Rapids, Michigan. He has written extensively on creation and cosmology from a Christian perspective.

A Revealed but Hidden God

CARL FEIT

How can professionally trained observers of nature view the same data and reach completely different conclusions as to what it all means?

A recent survey, reported in *Nature*, indicates that 40 percent of working scientists have a belief in a personal Deity. As a professional scientist, I find many of my colleagues are indeed devoted Jews, Christians, Muslims, Hindus, Buddhists, and others. But that is not to say our laboratories of molecular biology and particle physics are the breeding grounds for a massive new religious reawakening. I have other colleagues who are equally outspoken as atheists or as committed agnostics.

How does this disagreement come about?

Leading physicists, such as John Barrow and Paul Davies, argue that an accurate assessment of twentieth-century physics not only is compatible with religious thought but actually points to the necessity for the postulate that an Omnipotent and Purposive Creator is running the whole show. In a similar way, prominent biologists Arthur Peacocke and Elving Anderson have been led to make comparable claims based on an understanding of the forces behind evolution and an increased awareness of the exquisite complexity of the genomes of living organisms.

Over the past twenty-five years or so, such views have led to a relatively quiet but increasingly substantive dialogue among many scientists and religious thinkers. Together they are reevaluating the age-old question of the interface between science and religion.

Maimonides, the preeminent medieval Jewish thinker who was both a philosopher and a scientist, wrote the following:

There is a positive commandment to have love and awe for the Almighty God as it is written, "You shall love the Lord your God" (Deuteronomy 6:5). But by what method can one achieve this? When a human being contemplates [God's] great and awesome works (the Universe) and examines His creations, and from them he sees the unmeasurable wisdom and infinite capacities of the Creator, he will immediately be filled with love, and desire to praise and understand more about the Living God. (Mishnah Torah, Laws of Torah Fundamentals, 2:1)

It would seem that Maimonides shared the view of those modern scientists who feel that a deep and profound inspection of the world, with its intricate laws and patterns giving rise to both profound simplicity and remarkable complexity, is the correct and perhaps only way for a finite mind to develop love and appreciation for the infinite.

But on the other hand, what are we to make of those scientists who look out at the world and do *not* see it resonating with divine wisdom; those who see only a whimsical, probabilistic universe, driven onward by fate and chance? Can we ascribe their reactions to mere self-delusion and/or an obstinate will *not* to believe? Have they an a priori commitment to a materialistic universe without even a Blind Watchmaker in charge?

To throw some light on this we need a deeper insight into the character of the religious experience.

There is a beautiful hymn that is sung or recited at the Sabbath table during the third meal, as the holy day draws to a close. Written by a sixteenth-century Kabbalist, it begins: "God conceals Himself in the beauty of secrecy, the wisdom hidden from all conception."

Jewish thought has long recognized that while human beings long for the presence and company of God, it is often true that searching for the face of God can also be a frustrating experience. There are times when the world is undeniably a cold, hostile environment, not only lacking a suffusion of the warm love of God, but outwardly thwarting our most noble aspirations. We must understand that God at times hides his face.

This is fully acknowledged in the Bible; it is called *hester panim*. While it is true that there are times when God's guiding hand is abundantly apparent, as at the splitting of the Red Sea, there are also these periods of divine silence, as during the Holocaust.

Jewish rabbinic thinkers have extended this idea by introducing the idea of Tsimtsum or *contraction* to explain how a finite, material world can exist in the presence of an infinite, omnipresent Deity. In the act of creation, an all-powerful God had to contract and withdraw into himself, as it were, to make room for the finite physical world.

Since God "withdrew" in creating the universe, it is not surprising that there are no *obvious* footsteps leading back to God. Traditional Judaism is not tied nor necessarily committed to the validity of the Argument from Design. In fact, the Hebrew word for world or universe, *Olam*, is related to the root meaning "hidden"; God is, so to speak, *hidden* in this world. Our encounter with God is complex; it demonstrates a complementarity. As with the wave/particles of the quantum world, we are always exposed to the dual transcendent/immanent nature of the supreme Being.

As a staunchly committed Orthodox Jew and a professional immunologist, I am pleased that this new dialogue is taking place. I am convinced that holding a religious perspective can help us understand the spiritual dimension of science. Equally, I believe that grappling with scientific questions can help us achieve deeper insight into our religious traditions.

•

Carl Feit occupies the Ades Chair in Health Sciences at Yeshiva University in New York; he is involved in cancer research and is on the editorial board of Cancer Investigation. *Feit is also an ordained rabbi and Talmudic scholar.*

Meaning Makes a Comeback

GREGG EASTERBROOK

A few decades ago, the well-informed person might have said that by the end of the twentieth century, human thought would have disproved all ideals about meaning, purpose, or larger forces in life.

Science was assumed to be in the process of generating hard evidence that life is just replicating molecules and vibrating atoms, signifying nothing; existence itself a cosmic fluke, no more than a random burst of physics. A famous 1979 remark by the Nobel Prize physicist Steven Weinberg—"The more the universe seems comprehensible, the more it also seems pointless"—summed up the bleak view that was widely assumed to be settling in to dominate Western thought.

Literature, history, and philosophy were on similar tracks, drifting toward the "postmodern" view that there is no meaning and there are no fundamental truths—just a hodgepodge of claims that are all equally mistaken.

Instead, at the dawn of the new millennium, the concept of meaning is poised for a major comeback. Cosmologists, expected by now to possess proof that the genesis of the universe was just an aimless technical event, instead are uncovering ever more evidence that existence is shrouded in radiant mystery, and may be both infinite and eternal. Biologists, expected by now to possess proof that life is just a weird chemical accident, instead are uncovering ever more indications that the natural world is somehow prewired to make life probable. And literary thinkers, who would have expected that by now postmodern ennui would have routed all other schools of thought, instead are finding a striking revival of interest in religion, ethics, and the difference between right and wrong—the ideas associated with meaning.

Consider the emerging science of the Big Bang. Roughly twenty years ago, most scientists assumed that our universe burst forth by pure chance and someday will die, bringing existence itself to a depressing end. This is not the sort of picture that suggests any larger influence at work.

Today, however, the leading theory of the Big Bang, called "inflation" physics, holds that cogent physical laws were at work during the genesis; that entire galaxies can spring forth from microscopic pinpoints of seemingly empty space; and that new universes will arise forever, existence never knowing any conclusion. Theories like this reflect the same sort of majesty and wonder that religious creation stories have long insisted must have been present at the outset of the cosmos. Leading-edge thinkers in Big Bang physics now seem to have more in common with theologians than with the it's-all-pointless postmodern viewpoint. For instance, Allan Sandage, one of the world's preeminent astronomers, recently said that what seems to have happened at the Big Bang was so magnificent, it could only be understood as "a miracle."

Next consider the current state of the life sciences. Researchers continue to demonstrate that evolution works in organisms that already exist; no serious person any longer contests Charles Darwin's basic insight about environment causing adaptive change. But biologists have yet to come up with the vaguest explanation of how Darwinian mechanics could have created life. Because the ancient jump from inanimate to animate seems inexplicable, some scientists such as Stephen Jay Gould have maintained that human existence is a cosmic joke, so phenomenally unlikely as to be stripped of any claim to meaning.

Recently, however, thinkers associated with a new school of science usually called "complexity theory" have begun to produce evidence that the basic rules of chemistry, thermodynamics, and even mathematics have been ordered in ways that encourage both life and consciousness.

33

This doesn't prove there is a Creator behind the scenes: it's possible that life-favoring physical rules arose naturally. But the emerging notion of the physical world as fundamentally favorable to living things—that nature somehow "wants" us to be—may replace gloomy assumptions of life-as-fluke with a new view that incorporates a sense of living purpose.

As science comes to embrace more buoyant views of the human prospect, literature and philosophy may turn in this direction as well. Many contemporary literary thinkers espouse such despondent views of life because they assume that since science is busily proving existence to be meaningless, intellectuals must do the same. But it's a fallacy to assume that science has disproved larger influences. Charles Townes, a Nobel Prize–winning physicist and chief inventor of the laser beam, recently noted that "to think that science already knows enough to be certain there are no mystical forces is illogical." As the course of science shifts away from dispirited views of a senseless cosmos, toward a new vision of creation as poignantly favorable to life, then philosophy and literature will have to adjust. The recent upsurge of interest in metaphysics, or the theory of truth, is an indicator of such a transition.

One reason the boundary between science and religion is suddenly a hot topic again, after decades of being out of fashion, is that researchers are beginning to see signs of resplendence in the found world and are wondering what it all means. In the decades to come, science, which we all assumed would refute every spiritual belief, may instead emerge as a principal source of arguments that humanity is part of some larger, greater, and perhaps welcoming cosmic enterprise. New scientific evidence of resplendence may tell us that there is a God, or if not, that the purely natural cosmos is a far more auspicious place than was once guessed. Either way, an increasingly favorable view of the human prospect is suggested, one in which meaning makes a big comeback.

•

Gregg Easterbrook is a senior editor of the New Republic *and contributing editor to the* Atlantic Monthly. *His most recent book is* Beside Still Waters: Searching for Meaning in an Age of Doubt.

Part Three

Evolutionary Biology

Has Darwin's theory of evolution by natural selection made religious belief difficult and possibly even irrational? **Sam Berry** declares this not to be so. Creationists are misguided in attempting to disprove the findings of evolutionary science. Neither should believers fall back on a "God of the gaps" whose interventions supposedly account for those events that are as yet unexplained by science. Rather, religion and science should be seen as complementary—the former giving meaning to the otherwise blind mechanisms of the latter.

Arthur Peacocke points out that the initial reaction to Darwin's ideas was not as negative as popular legend would have us believe. Today we recognize even more clearly that the evolutionary process is an invitation to reflect on our understanding of God's ongoing relationship to the living world.

It is now widely accepted that much of our understanding and many of our attitudes have been profoundly shaped by the biological origins of our minds. This is likely to be as true of our religious beliefs as any other. Indeed, some evolutionists have tried to dismiss religious belief and practice as a mere stratagem encoded in our genes because it happens to confer some survival advantage. **Wentzel Van Huyssteen,** while rejecting this supposed "explaining away" of religion, nevertheless fully accepts that we need to take seriously the ways in which our attempts to understand God have been molded by the evolutionary origins of our minds. He sees this leading to rewarding conversations between religion and the sciences.

Barbara Smith-Moran addresses the question, "Which came first, God or human beings? Believers say God; it was he who created man. Atheists claim that people evolved first; God emerged only later as a human invention. Drawing upon the idea of coevolution (a bee and an orchid, for example, evolving together so that each species fits the other as a hand to a glove), Smith-Moran suggests this as a possible middle way of understanding the relationship between God and man.

Did Darwin Kill God?

SAM BERRY

For many, Charles Darwin is an ogre. With his theory of evolution by natural selection, he apparently destroyed the credibility of God. Is that true?

Science seems to tell us that the world is an enormous machine kept going by energy from the Sun, and that we are nothing but animals struggling to survive. To this way of thinking, God is unnecessary, or if he exists, irrelevant. Success in life depends solely on oneself. Religion is wishful thinking.

Not surprisingly, men and women of all religions react against such an assessment. They argue that it results from a distorted and incomplete understanding of life, the universe, and everything—an understanding that itself depends on faith. Some insist that the evidence for evolution is dangerous guesswork. They claim there is no compelling evidence for humans having evolved from apes. They point to gaps in the fossil record. They dismiss as faulty logic the notion that order and complexity could evolve through time contrary to the second law of thermodynamics, which shows the world to be running down. They point to the sacred writings (Bible, Quran, Vedas, and so on), which all insist that we are distinct from animals in a way that enables us to recognize and respond to spiritual forces.

Unfortunately for such attempts at a total rejection of Darwinian science, the evidence for evolutionary change is now overwhelming. Radioactive dating has shown that the world is billions of years old; we know that extinctions have occurred on a vast scale from the earliest times; and molecular biology has made it possible to compare species genetically in a way previously impossible—showing, for instance, that we humans differ from chimpanzees in fewer than 2 percent of our genes.

A rather more sophisticated way of keeping God around is to use him as an explanation for events that science cannot explain. The problem with this is that such a "God of the gaps" notion gets ever smaller as we learn more and more about the natural world. It smacks of the medieval belief that the soul must live in the pineal gland, because until recent times no one had yet figured out what the pineal gland did.

Attempts to consign science to the rubbish heap so as to find room for God are unnecessary. Aristotle recognized that any happening is likely to have more than one cause. For example, a painting is caused by the distribution of chemicals on a canvas, but it is just as much "caused" by the painter who had a plan for his work of art. We can describe the painting either in chemical (i.e., scientific) terms or as an artistic design: two completely different but noncontradictory explanations for the same thing.

God's work in creation and evolution can be described in exactly the same way. Reason tells me that evolution has taken place in the way Darwin described it, while my faith tells me that God governed the whole process. Indeed, the Bible suggests that the correct approach involves both God and science. In the New Testament we read that "through faith we understand that the world was framed by the word of God so that the things which are seen were made from those which are not seen." It is just as much an act of faith to believe that God did not make the world as it is to believe that he did. Unbelievers use faith as much as believers, although in an opposite direction.

It is a historic fact that most thinking people accepted evolution within a generation of Darwin's Origin of Species appearing. Some of the authors of the Fundamentals (1909–15), which were intended as definitive statements of orthodox Christianity, were entirely happy with the idea that God had used evolution as his method of creation.

What about the well-known debate between Bishop Samuel Wilberforce and T. H. Huxley in 1860? This was not really over science and religion. On the bishop's side it was about the danger of regarding change for its own sake as some kind of God. Churchgoing at the time was declining as workers moved from agriculture to factory life; attitudes toward the Bible were in a state of flux as its authority came under attack from "higher critics." Huxley's motives were entirely different; they were about removing the idea that the church should pronounce on science.

Other complicated agenda lay behind the Scopes "monkey trial" in Dayton, Tennessee, in 1925. The issue there was the nature of human beings as divine creations, not the occurrence of evolution as such. Modern creationism did not start from Darwin or from the original fundamentalists, but rather from Seventh-day Adventist George McCready Price, who claimed that Noah's flood so disrupted the geological record that orthodox geologists have been utterly misled. His turn-of-the-century views have been widely repeated and elaborated, but lack all scientific credibility.

As for the situation today, we find creationists claiming that evolutionists have been brainwashed by materialism, while evolutionists believe that creationists are muddleheaded in not accepting scientific reality. The tragedy is that the efforts of creationists to retain God as Creator by denigrating science are both misplaced and unnecessary.

There are proper scientific debates about whether Darwin's suggested mechanism of natural selection is adequate for explaining all the features of evolution, and there are continuing questions about the roots of human nature. But science and God, evolution and creation, are not alternatives. They are complements. The God of the Bible might well be a miracle worker on occasion, but normally he is to be seen at work through natural processes. It is God the Creator who gives meaning to the blind mechanisms of science.

•

Sam Berry is Professor of Genetics at University College London. He has been president of the Linnean Society, the British Ecological Society, the European Ecological Federation, and Christians in Science. In 1996, he received the Templeton UK Project Award. His books include Adam and the Ape *and* God and Evolution.

The Disguised Friend: Darwinism and Divinity

ARTHUR PEACOCKE

It would come as a surprise to many of the biologically cultured "despis-
ers of the Christian religion" to learn that historians are now showing
that the nineteenth-century reaction to Darwinism in theological and
ecclesiastical circles was much more positive and welcoming than the
popular legends have recounted up till now. Furthermore, the scientific
reaction was also, in fact, much more negative than is usually depicted.
Those skeptical of Darwin's ideas included initially the leading comparative anatomist of his day, Richard Owen, and the leading geologist,
Charles Lyell. Many theologians deferred judgment, but the proponents
of at least one strand in theology in nineteenth-century England chose
to intertwine their insights closely with those of Darwin. More of the
nineteenth-century religious reaction to Darwin was constructive and
reconciling in temper than practically any biological popularizers today
will allow.

The constructive approaches of those Christian thinkers who wished
to be reconcilers, rather than irreconcilers, between the new science and
Christian beliefs were not based on any mood of defeatism or any sense
of flabby compromise of Christian insights with new truths. They were
based on the conviction that, if the Christian faith is to be intelligible and
believable at all to each new generation, it must express itself in ways
that are consonant with such understandings as that generation has of
the world around it.

One could cite especially some of those in the "high" church tradition, with its emphasis on God working in the world and in persons
(technically, "incarnation"). Thus we have Aubrey Moore (1889):

*Darwinism appeared, and, under the disguise of a foe, did the work of a friend. It
has conferred upon philosophy and religion an inestimable benefit, by showing us*

43

that we must choose between two alternatives. Either God is everywhere present in nature, or He is nowhere.

In reflecting today on evolution, we recognize now, more than ever before, that new modes of existence, new activities, and new kinds of behavior come into existence through the course of evolutionary time — and that we need new concepts and ways of investigating them. New kinds of realities appear: increasing complexity, information processing, consciousness, and finally, in humanity, self-consciousness. So, the believer in God can affirm, with even greater conviction than before, that God is the *Continuous Creator*. He is all the time *creating* — through the processes of nature which the biologist uncovers. God makes things make themselves. The splendid panorama of both cosmic and biological evolution should be a stimulus to worship and awe.

Nevertheless, some (and it worried Darwin) have found it difficult to reconcile belief in God as Creator with the undoubted role of chance in the evolutionary process (mutations in the genetic carrier, DNA, are random with respect to the organism's environment, interaction with which "naturally" selects the best procreators). But we now know, through key developments in theoretical biology and physical biochemistry, that it is the *interplay of chance and law* that allows the matter of the universe to be self-creative of new forms of organization. God, whom the theist believes gives existence to the whole process, can now be conceived as creating *through* this interplay.

The results of this interplay display features that arise because they help survival: becoming more complex; gaining ability to process information about the environment (e.g., nerves) and to store it (e.g., brains) — so providing the basis for consciousness and self-consciousness, and for language needed in cooperation. Moreover, since new forms can only arise through the death of old ones, and because sensitivity is essential for survival, pain and death now appear as inevitable features of a biological world that is going to be creative of new forms, some of which can become conscious and self-conscious. Modern Christian thinkers conceive of God as suffering in, with, and under this process.

Within the continuities of these processes there arises Homo sapiens, a being who is undoubtedly a product of the natural process and yet has the mental capacity to know the process, and know that he or she knows —thereby evidencing an extraordinary distance from even the most intelligent primate or porpoise.

This panorama gives a new perspective for discussions of the traditional trio of "nature, humanity, and God"—an expansion of horizons for us all, especially believers in God. Moreover, insights of the religious, and indeed general, experience of humanity cannot be lightly set aside. For Homo sapiens is that creature which uniquely needs to come to terms with its awareness of death, with its finitude—needs to bear suffering, to realize its potentialities and to determine its path through life. It is to such needs that the religions of the world respond. Today that response must continue to be illuminated by the evolutionary perspective that Darwin so brilliantly began to unveil for humanity. We can now have, through his insights into the history of the living world, and those of countless biological scientists subsequently, a new, exhilarating vision of an ever-working Creator. He operates in, with, and under the dynamic processes of nature to bring forth the new until it culminates in human persons capable of self-offering love—persons open to values and to a harmonious relationship with the divine. For Christians, the vindication and warranty that their hope can be consummated are in the life,

45

death, and resurrection of the one human being fully exemplifying the culmination of the divine creative activity: Jesus the Christ.

•

Arthur Peacocke is the director of the Ian Ramsey Centre at Oxford University; a biologist; and founder of the Science and Religion Forum and of the Society of Ordained Scientists. His books include The Physical Chemistry of Biological Organization *and* God and Science: The Quest for Christian Credibility.

Evolution: The Key to Knowledge of God?

 WENTZEL VAN HUYSSTEEN

The process of evolution has shaped our world and our own species. It has also definitively shaped the way we *know* about this world. What does this imply for those who claim to know about God through religious belief and theological reflection?

Evolution by natural selection has traditionally, and famously, been regarded by many as a foe of Christian theology. As we progressively learn more about how the evolutionary pressures of the past affect the way our minds operate today, the theory now appears to be posing a new challenge to religion. While it has long been accepted that religious attempts to make sense of the meaning of our lives are embedded in and shaped by social, historical, and cultural factors, we now have to come to terms with the possibility that religious faith might also be shaped profoundly by the biological origins of our minds and of our self-awareness. This goes beyond the traditional challenge for Christian theology to take seriously biological evolution by natural selection.

Far from seeing this as a potential threat to religious belief, many Christian theologians are happy to accept the direct impact that our biological origins may have had on the way we think about religion, faith, and knowledge. They embrace this possibility convinced that the theory of evolution, far from attacking religion, could actually reveal something positive about the way religious believers claim to have knowledge about God.

Philosophers, of course, have long argued that human intelligence can be seen as naturally arising through evolutionary processes and as such provides us with one very effective way of survival. The question now is, Could the same be claimed for religion and religious faith?

Some neo-Darwinians have famously claimed that religion is just an extraneous "virus of the mind" and that distant religious "memories" of our species are not to be trusted. This position, however, does not take into account the amazing pervasiveness of religion through the ages. Certain Christian theologians are claiming that the universal prevalence of religious or metaphysical beliefs shows that they are closely related to the evolution of human cognition. On this view, metaphysical and religious beliefs are not at all in conflict with evolution, but are actually made intelligible by evolution.

For believers in a supernatural being, or God, this may have startling consequences: even if the theory of evolution by natural selection successfully precludes "deistic" or too "narrow" notions of God, it certainly does not by itself sufficiently explain religious belief or why some of us have faith in God.

These arguments from theologians who are trying to find ways to constructively appropriate evolutionary theory depend greatly on the claims of evolutionary epistemologists that all our different forms of knowledge are deeply integrated and embedded in the biological roots of the human mind. The basic assumption of evolutionary epistemology is, therefore, that we humans, like all other living beings, result from evolutionary processes and that, consequently, our mental capacities (our superior intelligence, our ability to construct metaphysical beliefs) are constrained and shaped by the mechanisms of biological evolution. What is now also argued, by at least some theologians, is that not only are all our different forms of human knowledge, especially scientific knowledge, firmly grounded in biological evolution, but also our claims to religious knowledge. On this view, the study of evolution becomes important not only for understanding the phenomenon of knowledge but also for understanding the claims of religious knowledge.

An even bolder assertion is that not only are metaphysical and religious beliefs in humans related to evolutionary processes, they now extend so hugely beyond biological evolution into cultural evolution that biology alone can no longer explain religion or religious faith.

The surprising result of this latter argument is that acceptance of an evolutionary account of the origin of human intelligence leaves ample scope for humans to develop meaning, values, and purpose (including religious meaning, values, and purpose) on a cultural level.

Christian theologians would rarely claim that this in any way constitutes an argument for God, or for the existence of God. What is claimed is that a responsible theological reinterpretation of these matters could make it clear why the idea of God, and of God's presence in this universe, could move us beyond well-known disputes like whether evolution operates through blind chance or providence, and whether "naturalism" or "supernaturalism" are really the only two narrow options open to Christian believers. This view asserts that evolution, rightly understood, can actually enrich our religious faith considerably, and may set the stage for a friendlier and more rewarding conversation between religion and the sciences.

No wonder, then, that the impact of the theory of evolution is again today felt far beyond the boundaries of biology. What is different, though, is that for some theologians at least, much of the earlier animosity and conflict between science and religion is fast disappearing. By revealing the biological origins of all our knowledge—including our religious knowledge—evolutionary epistemology becomes a handy tool for theologians who are looking for a meaningful interdisciplinary dialogue with the sciences. Within the context of this conversation, God and natural selection do not have to be competing hypotheses anymore. For the Christian theologian God's presence in our universe seems to be the best explanation of progress toward greater consciousness and intentionality in the evolution of life on Earth.

For the Christian believer the experience of religious faith has always profoundly mediated a personal presence. The experience of this presence obviously cannot prove the existence of God. It does, however, have far-reaching implications: it places religious belief within a wider set of general beliefs about the natural world, and it shows how it may integrate coherently with them.

•

Wentzel Van Huyssteen is Professor of Theology and Science at Princeton Theological Seminary in Princeton, New Jersey; he was formerly head of the Department of Religion at the University of Port Elizabeth in South Africa. Among his books is Rethinking Theology and Science: Six Models for the Current Discussion.

The Evolutionary Past and Future of God

BARBARA SMITH-MORAN

Are we created in God's image, as the Bible tells it? Or is it the other way around, as nonbelievers say? This question grows out of the study of human evolution, and it never fails to cut short a good conversation about religion. Ask the riddle about the chicken or the egg, and everyone chuckles. Religion, however, is no laughing matter. Just ask whether God or human beings came first, and people will argue until they're red in the face. It's clear that this question matters, and matters a lot.

How did our world come to be the way it is, anyhow? The Bible gives one version. Modern biology tells another. Agreement between the two seems impossible at first glance. But a deeper look shows that science can suggest fresh thinking about God and creation.

In the Bible's opening act, God plays the starring role of Creator "in the beginning." According to a master script in six acts, things start to appear on stage at God's command. Light first, then rain and rivers, oceans, land and plants, Sun and Moon, fish and birds. Wild animals and human beings top the job off, and then God takes a Sabbath Day rest. That's the religious story, for Jews and Christians.

But today there is another creation story. The story of evolution tells us that it happened a different way. Nothing appeared suddenly at the command of a Creator. Instead, things took form over billions of generations, developing slowly from ancient forms that are no longer around. Plants and animals just evolved—humans included.

Some people then go on to add that, last of all, onto the stage came God—a human invention on a par with the wheel, the plow, and the domesticated pig. All inventions fill a need, and this one was to fill the need for an ally to control the forces of nature—storms, earthquakes, and famines.

In this way, there arises our dichotomy: was God there "in the beginning," or only at the end of the process? I believe there is a middle way.

Evolution is the brainchild of the nineteenth-century scientists Alfred Russel Wallace and Charles Darwin. At one time the crude image of a battle for "the survival of the fittest" was thought to be the best way to understand evolution. But today, scientists know that things work far more subtly. They see the role of cooperation, not competition alone, as key to the way evolution works.

Long-term cooperation—really long term, say millions of years—gives rise to something called "coevolution." This happens when two species—an orchid and a bee, for instance—stay together over so many generations that each one has helped to shape the way the other one looks. It is amazing to see how the inside of a given orchid flower fits snugly around the only bee that can pollinate it. Not too big and not too small. As if by design, the two species fit perfectly together, like hand in glove. The outside of the bee is the "image" of the inside of the orchid, even though this is not how things looked eons ago.

So which came first, the orchid or the bee? The answer is both! They "grew up" together, evolved together. Put it this way: the bee is the "creator" of its favorite orchid. And the reverse is equally true: the orchid "created" its favorite bee. This is an example of the new "systems thinking" in biology.

This new idea suggests a breakthrough in the standoff about God and man, and who created whom, and in whose image. Could it be that God and people coevolved? Could it be that their close partnership is the fruit of long-term—really long term—cooperation? Such questions could open up fresh and interesting conversations between believers in creation and believers in evolution.

New discoveries in science can often lubricate the sticking points in our understanding of God. The coevolution of orchids and bees suggests that God and people might be creators of each other. Neither would have a monopoly on the creative power. Neither would have an exclusive claim to be the "creature."

It also suggests that God and people have a need for one another. The bee needs the orchid nectar for food, but what's the payoff of the partnership for the orchid? Well, if the flower parts are arranged just so, the bee has to wade through pollen to get at the nectar. The dusty bee then brushes pollen off on the female flower parts at the next nectar stop. And bingo! Pollination.

So it's possible that God needs human hands and voices to carry out the divine hopes for the world. It's possible that people need God's "long view" and wisdom concerning justice and peace, balance and beauty, life and death.

The bee and the orchid looked different in the past, before their million-year "marriage." The same might be said of God and people. Perhaps the "early God" was less focused in human affairs back in early times. Perhaps our own ancestors in the prehuman mists were only dimly aware of any God at all.

Looking to the future is just as intriguing. Nature shows that many coevolved species continued to became better suited to each other. Some partners became totally dependent on each other for survival. We can only speculate on how God and people might work together in their linked evolutionary future.

•

Barbara Smith-Moran is the founding director of the Center for Faith and Science Exchange at Boston Theological Institute in Boston, Massachusetts; her training is in biology and chemistry, and she has an M.A. in astronomy. Smith-Moran is an ordained Episcopal priest and is cochairperson of the Episcopal Church Working Group on Science, Technology, and Faith.

Part Four

Life in the Universe

Confronted with the vast numbers of stars revealed to us by modern-day telescopes—each star a sun, many accompanied by planets—it is natural to assume that life-forms at least as intelligent as humans must have evolved elsewhere. Before jumping to that conclusion, however, **Christopher Kaiser** points out that conditions here on Earth are very special. We could conceivably be the only species in the cosmos capable of doing science and of wondering why we are here.

Robert Jastrow accepts that humans might indeed be unique, but he goes on to explore some of the implications of discovering life elsewhere. Because evolutionary times are long, and we are but relatively recent arrivals on the scene, if there is life out there, some of it is likely to be vastly more advanced than we are; in the cosmic order our position is likely to be humble. Extraterrestrial life might be ahead of us not only in terms of science but also in terms of morals, ethics, and religious beliefs. God surely will be as much interested in them as in us.

But what will alien life-forms be like? Media portrayals of them vary from the angelic to the demonic. **Robert Russell** examines the possibilities and concludes with the prediction that, should we meet them one day, we shall find that they conform to neither of these extremes; they will be a lot like us, seeking the good but beset by failures.

Willem Drees asks whether the coming of the Son of God in the specific form of Jesus on Earth can any longer be regarded as having cosmic significance, given the possibility of life elsewhere. Perhaps we need to think more modestly about Jesus. Aliens are likely to have their own sets of traditions and stories. God's love will have been made known to them in their own way. And yet it is to be expected that there will be an affinity between our beliefs and theirs.

Zaki Badawi reminds us that the Islamic tradition, while not according Jesus the status characteristic of orthodox Christian thinking, nevertheless venerates him.

Are We Alone?

Are we alone in the cosmos? Or are there living beings out there just waiting to make contact? Could they be watching us now with their telescopes? Or is that vast sky of stars around us nothing but gas and dust? We may be able to answer some of these questions.

One thing we know for sure. There are billions and billions of stars out there. But life cannot possibly exist on the stars themselves. They are so hot that all liquids boil away. Still, there could be lots of planets. Our Sun is like lots of other stars. So there should be plenty of stars with planets in the sky. Astronomers have discovered more than a dozen of them so far. The discovery of a new planet is being announced almost every month. If any of these have water on them, simple life forms could exist. They could be infested with bacteria.

What about larger creatures like fish and dinosaurs? This is a more difficult question. Suppose that evolution is nature's way of making plants and animals. This process requires long periods of time and stable temperatures. But most planets have chaotic orbits. Slowly but surely they spin around in strange ways. Then they get either too hot or too cold for most plants and animals.

In other words, nature is like a huge house of cards. A good shake will bring them all down. So do not expect all of those planets to have bones or footprints on them. They may harbor bacteria in nooks and crannies. But they are not anything like Jurassic Park.

Still, somewhere there may be a planet with stable conditions like ours. Then large plants and animals might have enough time to evolve. But there would not be spaceships and telescopes. Even if a planet has stable temperatures, it is not likely to have intelligent life on it, at least not the kind of intelligence that is needed for the pursuit of science and technology.

There are many different kinds of intelligence. Experts have identified at least six kinds in humans alone. Many other species of life are also intelligent, but they do not use computers. Chimps are intelligent in their own way, but they do not do mathematics. Whales have a language of their own, but they do not study astronomy. Out of the millions of species on Earth, only humans even try to do math and science. Only humans use electricity and build telescopes. Maybe there are creatures on other planets that can walk or even talk. Still, they are not likely to build computers and spaceships.

All the planets astronomers have found so far are large ones like Jupiter. That is just because giant planets are easier to locate than small ones like Earth. The giant planets are too cold for water to flow on their surface. They are all made of frozen gases like Jupiter. But for each of those giants there must be several smaller planets and plenty of moons. Here temperatures might be right for growing bacteria. The stars are too hot. The giant planets are too cold. But the smaller planets and moons could be just about right. Even here on Earth bacteria are found living in places that are very hot or very cold. There are fountains of boiling water at the bottom of the oceans. Special types of bacteria can live there. Others eke out an existence deep in the ice of Antarctica. One-celled creatures can exist under extreme conditions like that. But we cannot, nor can other plants and animals. That is why nature is like a house of cards. If the temperatures change very much the larger plants and animals die off.

So why were plants and animals able to survive on Earth? If it is so difficult to get stable temperatures, why are we so lucky? If most planets and moons are chaotic, why is our Earth so stable? The reason is that we have the Moon. The Moon is large enough to raise tides and to make Earth's orbit stable. No other planet in the solar system has moons big enough to do that. And none of the planets in outer space is likely to have such a moon either.

Scientists have tried to program the birth of the Moon on computers. The only way to get a Moon as large as ours is to have a huge asteroid splash into the surface of the Earth. Then tons of stuff get blasted out into space. If the asteroid is the right size and if it grazes the Earth at just the right angle, enough stuff is blasted out to form the Moon. It is difficult to reproduce a birth like that. Sure, there are plenty of planets and moons out in space. But it is not likely that any planet has a moon large enough to keep its orbit stable.

Good planets are hard to find. And humans are unique. But the question is not why there is no extraterrestrial intelligence. The question is why intelligence exists here on Earth. Why are we able to do science and create technology? Why are we here at all? Perhaps just so there will be someone around to think about these things. If we are part of a divine plan, that kind of thinking must be very important to the Creator.

•

Christopher Kaiser is Professor of Historical and Systematic Theology at Western Theological Seminary in Holland, Michigan; he holds doctorates in astro-geophysics and in theology. Among his books is Creation and the History of Science.

A Cosmic Perspective on Human Existence

ROBERT JASTROW

Reports of fossil life on Mars, if confirmed by a Mars landing, are of enormous significance. Until now, it has been possible to believe that the evolution of life out of nonlife, even if scientifically explainable, is an event of such vanishingly small probability as to be essentially a miracle. There has been no scientific evidence to support what Carl Sagan used to call the "principle of mediocrity," which asserts that *if life appeared on this ordinary planet, why would it not appear on similar planets elsewhere?* Contrary to the principle of mediocrity, the evidence has been consistent with the belief that inhabited planets are extremely rare; we may be alone in the universe.

Fred Hoyle estimates the a priori probability of life assembling out of inanimate matter to be one in ten raised to the one hundred millionth power. The biochemist Robert Shapiro estimates it more optimistically to be one in 10^{992}. Since there are only at most some billion trillion (i.e., 10^{21}) planets circling sunlike stars in the known universe, both estimates mean that we are alone.

Now the significance of the tentative discovery of Martian fossils becomes clear. The recent reports of a number of planets circling nearby stars suggest that planets are common and trillions exist in the observable universe. The discovery of Martian life or fossils would indicate that the appearance of life on these planets cannot be a rare event. If it were, planets with life would be thinly scattered in the universe and we would certainly not find two of these very rare objects—a planet with life—in the same solar system. The discovery of life on Mars would imply that many of the trillions of planets in the known universe are inhabited. The universe must be teeming with life.

Furthermore, since the universe is about 15 billion years old, give or take a few billion years, and the Earth is only 4.5 billion years old, many of these inhabited planets must be far older, and possibly further along in their evolutionary development, than we are. It follows that we are relatively recent arrivals in the cosmos. Intelligent life in other solar systems, if it exists (for which we have as yet no proof), is likely to be superior to us in its scientific and technical knowledge.

The message in these scientific findings is clear. Although humans stand at the summit of creation on this planet, in the cosmic order our position is humble.

Will it be wise to make contact with forms of life so far above us? There are risks. In the contact between scientifically advanced civilizations and a primitive society—and such is the description we must apply to ourselves as we prepare to enter the galactic community—it is the usual lot of the less developed peoples to be destroyed by the encounter, as powerful forces at the command of the technically advanced civilization tear apart the fabric of the primitive society.

These have been the consequences of exposure to a more advanced technology for Neolithic civilizations on the Earth, when only a few thousand years of cultural evolution separate the two societies. What may be expected from a meeting between civilizations separated by many millions of years of evolution? Can humankind survive the shock of the encounter? I see no grounds for optimism.

To return to the basic theme: its elements can be briefly stated. Science, particularly astronomy, has created a new perspective on humanity—the cosmic perspective on human existence. First, we know that we are relative newcomers in the universe. Therefore, if life exists elsewhere, most of it is far older and conceivably more advanced than Homo sapiens. Second, we now have evidence that Earth may be one of many trillions of planets in the known universe. Third, the Earth appears to be a very ordinary sort of planet, made of materials common in the universe. It does not seem likely that this very ordinary planet should be the only one among trillions that has been the scene of the emergence of life. If life is indeed common on those trillions of planets, humanity is only a speck floating in a cosmic sea of intelligent life.

Is there a larger meaning to this picture of a universe teeming with life? If true, it can only be described as an explosion of creative power. What is the purpose of this creative power? Is there a life force in the cosmos that must express itself in this way? Again, what is the purpose of it all? It would seem to be without purpose, but that answer leaves one dissatisfied. We want to know the larger meaning in this. There must be a meaning, but what is it? If science cannot tell us, we are compelled to look elsewhere. But where? For those holding the materialist-reductionist view of life, there is nowhere else to look. This notion is depressing.

Finally, a more specifically theological issue: Paul Johnson, a British historian, suggests that as Judeo-Christian values were superior to those of paganism, with its human sacrifice and other pernicious practices, advanced extraterrestrial life-forms may have a form of monotheism superior to Judeo-Christian beliefs. If so, they may be at least as worthy of God's interest as we are. Indeed, some of the older races might be not only scientifically more advanced, but also superior in their moral and ethical values and religious beliefs. Does this not create problems for the traditional Judeo-Christian view of the Deity as being very much concerned with the affairs of the particular race of intelligent beings that exists on our planet?

A logically impeccable answer is that the Deity is omnipotent and can be concerned with the affairs of as many intelligent races on as many planets as the Deity wishes. But it seems to me that the image of a God whose attention is divided among trillions of intelligent races inevitably dilutes the relationship between God and humankind which is the essence of the Old and New Testaments.

If and when the communication with advanced life occurs, I believe these implications will have a transforming effect on Western religion, requiring far greater adjustments in theological thought than those prompted by the discovery that the Earth revolves around the Sun or even the evidence in the fossil record that seems to link humans to simpler forms of life.

•

Robert Jastrow is director of the Mount Wilson Institute in southern California. He was the founding director of NASA's Goddard Institute for Space Studies and the first chairman of NASA's Lunar Exploration Committee. He was formerly Professor of Earth Sciences at Dartmouth College in Hanover, New Hampshire. Jastrow has hosted more than one hundred CBS network television programs.

What Are Extraterrestrials Really Like?

ROBERT RUSSELL

When I was a kid, I was determined to be the first person to land on Mars. I wanted to meet the Martians: would they be like us, or incredibly different? Hollywood showed us one answer: *War of the Worlds* extraterrestrial life was here, not to talk, but to conquer! Things haven't changed much with today's cinema. There are *Aliens* (plus its sequels), *Star Wars*, and *Star Trek*—and the cute, cuddly, angelic E.T. But where's the truth in all the celluloid packaging?

The truth might be "stranger than you think." Some scientists are looking for evidence of primitive life in our own solar system. As recently as 1997, scientists at NASA thought they had found evidence of early forms of life on Mars, taken from meteorites that had been knocked off the Red Planet and eventually trapped by Earth's gravity to land in the arctic wastelands. We all saw the photos of those worm-like fossils— more like pasta than plasma! And they were terribly small, too. So the comparison with Earth life was limited at best. Still, what if . . . ?

There's less enthusiasm now for the Martian sample, but there's still a buzz about life in the universe. European and American space agencies are considering an unmanned landing on the surface of Europa, that icy moon of Jupiter. Beneath its vast oceans, whose surface is permanently frozen, there could be just the right conditions for primitive life to evolve. Will we undertake the mission? I hope so!

Other scientists are exploring the possibility of advanced life having already evolved on the planets of nearby stars—and we almost daily discover evidence of those planets. At the distances involved, it's not likely that we'll send a probe there, but we can listen with our radio telescopes to see if life out there is signaling us: " We're here!" This is exactly the mission of the Search for Extraterrestrial Intelligence (SETI) project.

Let's just suppose that someday we discover a signal, like in Carl Sagan's extraordinary movie, Contact. What could we hope to learn from the encounter?

For starters, we'll learn whether intelligent life throughout the universe reasons the way we do, say, by writing down the same laws of physics. Or perhaps the way we reason is tied up with the specific evolutionary history of our species, and extraterrestrials will think in ways we can't even recognize!

Now for a tough one: if they reason like us, will they also make moral decisions? The philosopher Michael Ruse says that our moral codes are bequeathed us by evolution. The biologist Francisco Ayala disagrees: we evolved the capacity for moral choice, but the particular values we hold are "free variables," and we can choose among options. What about extraterrestrial life?

Let's go one step further: suppose ETs are moral creatures, who consider and act with the best of intentions. Will they be able to pull it off and be "angelic," as Sagan imagined? Or will they, like us, be conflicted with profound moral dilemmas? St. Augustine predicted that all humanity would "sin"; we will never find people on Earth leading an entirely blessed life. What about extraterrestrial life? Is our penchant for wickedness just the result of something that went tragically wrong on Earth as life and intelligence evolved? Or is it built into the very fabric of life, something which no intelligent creature can avoid, whose past, like ours, is the trail of death and extinction that marks the long, arduous evolutionary journey to mind and values?

Since we've come this far on our little thought experiment, let's go one step further. What about hope? Suppose ETs are not that different from us after all: grasping for the good, the true, the beautiful, yet thwarted by "clay feet," mired in moral ambiguity. Will God provide a pathway of healing, saving grace for ETs as God has done for us humans on Earth? This is, of course, the horizon-breaking image of the "cosmic Christ" which Pierre Teilhard de Chardin envisioned and which continues to inspire many of us today.

Let's close with an empirical prediction which I'll make on the basis of Christian theology—surely a rarity for theologians! I predict that when we finally make contact with life in the universe, it will be neither the insipidly angelic E.T. variety nor the unmitigated demonic alien that *Independence Day* portrays. Instead, I predict that it will be a lot like us: seeking the good, beset by failures, and open to the grace of forgiveness and new life that God offers all God's creatures, here or way out there. In short, I predict that the discovery of extraterrestrial life will "hold a mirror up" to us and we will see someone not unlike ourselves, filled with questions like ours and beckoning to us in hopes of discovering the answers, too. And I predict that, against those voices who say life in the universe is meaningless, or that human life is absurd, we'll be able to recognize the common journey of life everywhere, and we will finally be able to understand our place in the Universe. Welcome home, humanity! Welcome home, ET!

•

Robert Russell is Professor of Theology and Science at the Graduate Theological Union in Berkeley, California; he is also the founder and director of the Center for Theology and the Natural Sciences in Berkeley. In addition to being a physicist, Russell is an ordained minister in the United Church of Christ.

Bethlehem: Center of the Universe?

WILLEM B. DREES

Extraterrestrials may be discovered in this new millennium. How would this affect belief in God? And would there not be a serious problem over the significance of Jesus in relation to these other inhabited worlds?

Philipp Melanchthon, a reformer with Martin Luther, wrote in 1550 that it would be improper to assume that Jesus Christ died more than once. Nor should one imagine that inhabitants of other worlds could be saved without having known the Son of God.

That being so, one idea might be to spread the Gospel via radio and television throughout the cosmos. Quite a project for televangelists! But this is hardly a realistic prospect — given the large distances involved. In any case, it is unsatisfactory to regard faith as though it were merely a matter of transferring information. After all, would we ourselves be inspired by information about a six-legged blue person on some planet X many light-years away?

In the past millennium we have abandoned the idea that the Earth is physically at the center of the cosmos. And yet we still often place ourselves at the center of significance. This is clearly the case in Christianity, where Jesus is believed to have cosmic significance. Such a claim makes the Earth theologically unique.

In my opinion we need to think more modestly about Jesus. The Bible itself warns against hubris. Jesus was not born in Rome or in Jerusalem, but in lowly Bethlehem. Not in a palace but in a stable. According to the creeds, he is assumed to be genuinely human, flesh of our flesh and bone of our bones, as well as revelatory of God. What does this say to us in the age of space travel and the Internet?

The issue is not that he provided us with new information. Faith is not about data that can be spread on the World Wide Web and throughout the cosmos. The significance of his life can perhaps be better expressed with a metaphor borrowed from biology. A German scholar of the New Testament, Gerd Theissen, spoke of Jesus as a mutation in cultural history. This somewhat unusual suggestion was prompted by the fact that mutations create new possibilities. The first feeble legs brought life to the land. The development of warm-blooded creatures led to the first experience of the wonder of a cold, starry night. In the same way, Jesus opened up new possibilities in regard to our relationship with the divine and with each other.

Of course, every image has its limitations. So, too, this image of Jesus as a mutation. Solidarity with the poor and the weak calls into question the selective process that drives evolution. The message and example of Jesus are that, in the end, solidarity does more justice to reality than selection. Or, to say it in the language of faith: God's grace is more important than God's judgment. Jesus goes against the exclusion of strangers. He speaks of love for one's enemy. At the cross, the helpless one is claimed to be Lord of All; the victim is the priest.

So, what about persons on other planets? They will not know of incarnation or crucifixion. They will not have a Bible in Hebrew and Greek. For them there is no story of someone beaten on the road from Jericho to Jerusalem—and then helped by a stranger rather than by a priest of his own tribe.

But this is not to say that the idea of love has not been radicalized there as well. They too, in their better moments, could have the sense that one should not only love one's family or friends, but one should also see the stranger and the enemy as neighbors.

There will be no story of a son who has squandered his inheritance and has to take care of pigs. But there may well be a message of forgiveness. Just as "the lost son" was allowed to return home, there might be other stories of new beginnings. The language and the images will be quite different. Convictions and values might be different, too. And yet one may hope for a deep affinity.

A lover says to the beloved, "You are the loveliest," and together they travel in trust and love. But no investigation on Earth and beyond has been made to justify that statement; no cosmic claim is being asserted.

So too will religious language always be close to our hearts. Christians have a particular story as the one most important for them. Jesus Christ is the center of their faith and of their lives. But that is not to say that extraterrestrials are to be conformed to traditional theological schemes; Bethlehem does not have to be the center of the universe. It is more important to be open-minded, loving, and responsible.

Extraterrestrial company is a challenge for Christian theology. However, this challenge should be welcomed. Just as we don't like to be accused of racism or sexism, so too we should find planetism unacceptable. We on Earth cannot assume to be closer to God than they are.

In my opinion, the existence of life elsewhere would pose no particular problem for traditional beliefs about God. According to the tradition, God already cares for all humans—six billion of them—as well as for birds. That sounds like quite a challenge. But God is believed to surpass human limitations. Omnipotence and omnipresence are among his attributes. The discovery of extraterrestrial life should therefore add no new problems in this respect. The sciences challenge belief in God in various ways, but this is not one of them.

Willem Drees is Professor of the Philosophy of Nature and Technology at the University of Twente in the Netherlands; he also conducts research into the science/ religion interface at Vrije Universiteit in Amsterdam. Drees is the author of Beyond the Big Bang: Quantum Cosmologies and God *and* Religion, Science, and Naturalism.

Jesus in Islam

ZAKI BADAWI

Muslims do not accept that Jesus was the Son of God. So, how do they in fact regard him?

The Qur'an stresses the background to Jesus' birth, starting from the birth of his mother Mary. The Qur'an tells us that Mary's mother, when she was pregnant, vowed that the child she was carrying would be a consecrated offering to God. Clearly, her hope was that she would give birth to a boy. She was disappointed to have a girl. But she prayed to God that her daughter would be protected from Satan and that she would be an accepted offering to God. Allah answered the prayer by later sending an angel to say, "O Mary, behold Allah has elected thee and made thee pure and raised thee above all women of the world."

Mary, chosen by God to be Jesus' mother, withdrew from her family to an Eastern place and kept herself in seclusion. The Qur'an states: "Whereupon We sent unto her Our angel of revelation." The angel declared to her, "I am a messenger from thine Sustainer Who says that I shall bestow upon thee a son endowed with purity." She replied, "How can I have a son when no man has ever touched me? For never have I been a loose woman."

The story moves on to the time of Jesus' birth. When people accused Mary of immorality, she pointed to the baby, who at once spoke, saying, "I am a servant of God. He has vouchsafed unto me revelation and made me a prophet and made me blessed wherever I may be."

Thus the story of Jesus' miraculous conception and birth is featured in the Qur'an. The Qur'an argues, however, that having no father is not proof of divinity—in the case of Jesus—any more than having no parents at all is evidence of Adam's divinity. The rigorous monotheism enshrined within Islam has no place whatever for any Trinitarian doctrine. Indeed, the career of Jesus is not mentioned in detail in the Qur'an

71

beyond that he called upon his people to worship the one God. He also released the Jews from certain food prohibitions, which the Qur'an says were imposed on them as a punishment for their disobedience.

The other crucial presentation of Jesus in the Qur'an centers on the crucifixion. The Qur'an denies that it took place and states that those who claimed to have crucified him were confused. The Qur'an informs us that Allah gathered Jesus to Himself and lifted him up (*Rafa'ahu*) to be in His presence. There is a dispute among Muslim commentators on the Qur'an as to whether Jesus was dead as he was lifted up to heaven. Some believe him to be still alive with God and that he will die only at the end of time.

The denial of the crucifixion is not meant simply as a rejection of the fact of crucifixion, but perhaps it is meant also as a denial of the whole idea of a savior and redeemer. The relationship between man and God in Islam has no room for the need for such redemption. Every individual is responsible for his or her actions. The sins of the fathers are not visited upon the children.

Jesus in the tradition of the prophet Muhammad is venerated to such a degree as to accord him and his mother a unique place in Muslim belief. The tradition says that every newborn is prodded by the devil except Jesus and his mother, Mary.

But the most important development in the tradition refers to the second coming of Jesus. Muslim eschatology has a place for Jesus to return and proclaim the absolute unity of the transcendental God.

The tradition portrays Jesus as a prophet guiding his people toward understanding God as merciful. He is described as the prophet of mercy. This picture of him influenced the mystic writers and practitioners who modeled themselves on him as humble, forgiving, and caring servants of God.

Sufi literature abounds with quotations from Jesus emphasizing God's forgiveness and mercy. The theologians regard him as the second stage in an evolutionary process beginning with Moses, who addressed the tyranny of Pharaoh and the obduracy of the Jews with the overwhelming power of a vengeful God. In contrast to Moses, Jesus brought the concept of the forgiving God, who readmits the repentant to the fold. The final stage of the evolution comes with Muhammad, who combines both concepts of God the Vengeful and the Merciful, the God of justice and forgiveness.

In popular Islam, Jesus and Mary occupy an important place in the imagination of the people. It is not unusual for Muslims to report the vision of Mary appearing in the sky at times of crisis as if to comfort the bereaved and to reassure the frightened and to give hope to the despairing.

Legends about Jesus' tolerance in the face of aggression, and kindness to the weak and needy, are transmitted orally in gatherings of worshipers by preachers and storytellers. Jesus, the friend of the meek and the helper of the afflicted, is always appealed to as an example to those full of pride and devoid of kindness.

The prophet Muhammad is linked closely with Jesus as carrying on the same message of God's unity and the unity of the human race. Jesus sought to free the Jews from their tribalism, and so did Muhammad with the Arabs, and indeed with the rest of humankind.

●

Zaki Badawi is the Principal of the Muslim College in London.

Part Five

 Genes and Genetic Engineering

Evolution involves the natural selection of certain genes. Genetic studies have enjoyed much success in recent years, to the extent that some biologists now claim humans to be nothing but by-products of the actions of these "selfish genes." **Keith Ward** disagrees. He sees them as part of a code written by a supreme Mind. **Elving Anderson** and **John Habgood** likewise warn against simplistic interpretations. The interlocking complexities of the circumstances under which genes operate mean that we are more than our genes. Not only that, the overall picture remains consistent with there being divine purpose.

The genes are now known to be encoded in the DNA molecule. The Human Genome Project aims to map out all these codes, identifying the function of each. Having done this, it becomes possible to modify their structure, thus giving rise to alternative behavior. **Ted Peters** raises the question of whether this is desirable or not. Clearly a strong case can be made for the irradication of diseases arising from malfunctioning genes. But what of other applications of genetic engineering? We must choose — and choose we can; though genetically influenced, we retain our free will.

Celia Deane-Drummond sees genetic manipulation allowing us to control how a species develops; we can even move genes from one species to another. This offers both promise — and risk. We need to proceed cautiously, showing respect for the creature, keeping in mind the whole picture, and remaining alert to our own motives. Human creativity is a gift from God. We have here the potential to become cocreators with God — but only if we act wisely.

Finally, **Michael Northcott** addresses the particularly contentious issue of the cloning of humans. The prospect is raised of genetically engineering a race of perfect superhumans through the creation of "designer babies." But is this what we want? Would it not be better to save our genetic inheritance in its flawed but still wondrous diversity?

Gene Wars

KEITH WARD

There is a war between science and religion. At least, there is a group of scientists and philosophers who lose no opportunity to attack belief in God as infantile and as incompatible with scientific knowledge. Among the most vocal are a number of neo-Darwinian biologists. They claim that evolutionary biology shows that religious faith is a genetically imprinted belief which had survival value in the past. Human persons are accidental by-products of blind material processes. Minds and bodies are anarchistic federations of selfish genes.

However, it is not biology which establishes these claims. It is rather a dogmatic materialism which interprets the biological evidence in a slanted way. Religious faith may indeed have survival value, but that does not imply that it is false. The evidence for God is not objective experiment but personal experience. The refusal to count personal experience as evidence is simply a dogma of materialism.

For the religious believer, God is not an entity slipped into gaps in the empirical world. God is a spiritual presence and value who can be sensed in and through all things. Of course, the investigation of nature should tell us something about God—in fact it seems to show how beautiful, intelligible, elegant, and intricate the structure of the natural world is, and thereby how intelligent and powerful its Creator is.

How could evolutionary biology throw doubt on this? Only by showing that the evolutionary process is one of blind chance or accident, so that it could not have been created by a God for a purpose. For most physicists, there is no such thing as "blind chance" in nature, which is why physicists are rarely as dogmatic as evolutionary biologists. But one main ploy of the neo-Darwinians is to eliminate all signs of purpose from the evolutionary process, by making purposes a by-product of blindly selfish behavior by millions of genes. Genes may indeed be blind, since they have no awareness. But how then can they be called "selfish"?

The poetic metaphor of the "selfish gene" is a powerful one, but its defects are greater than its inventor, Richard Dawkins, allows. In his latest book, he concedes that genes express their selfishness by means of cooperating with other sets of genes—which sounds like what Humpty Dumpty (for whom words can mean whatever he wants them to) might mean by "selfishness." The basic fact behind the selfish gene metaphor is that sequences of DNA replicate, and that some sequences replicate efficiently while others do not, largely because of environmental conditions favoring their survival. The fact behind the "selfish cooperator" metaphor is that the most efficient replicating sequences will often be those which form parts of larger organisms, constructed by the cooperative activity of many sequences of DNA.

Of course, genes also mutate. Indeed, mutation is essential to the development of those more complex forms of organic life in which genes might flourish. A truly selfish gene would not wish to mutate, but would wish to keep its sequence intact. Only an altruistic gene would be happy to mutate, giving up its life for some better future. At that point, however, it may be better to stop suggesting that genes are either selfish or unselfish.

The most important fact about genes is that they produce the proteins which build bodies. They are recipes for constructing parts of bodies. As such, they need to cooperate with other genes to get their job done—and of course they also need to mutate (and therefore to die) if bodily improvements are ever to occur. What the metaphor of the selfish gene does is to lead the unsuspecting reader to think that persons are by-products of tiny self-serving strings of molecules. Whereas faced with the biological facts, most people might think that the production of organic bodies, and ultimately of persons, is precisely the reason DNA recipes should exist at all.

It would certainly be odd if some reductionist cook should claim that cakes are an accidental by-product of the desire of selfish recipes to reproduce themselves as widely as possible. Once one sees genes as "recipes," or informational codes (which is what they are), the attraction of calling them "selfish" may begin to fade.

It is better, perhaps, to eliminate the metaphor and marvel at the truly amazing order and design of the genetic code, which brings persons into being by incredibly elegant natural processes over many thousands of generations. Genes are neither selfish nor cooperative. But it would not be too difficult to see them as parts of an intricate and elegant code written into the atomic structure of matter itself by a supreme Mind, with the purpose of generating responsible and intelligent persons from unconscious and unthinking material.

Evolutionary biology is an exciting and mind-expanding subject. It would be sad if it became too closely associated with irrational attacks on a spiritual perception of the world. It promises a better understanding of the rational structure of the world. It promises to expand human responsibility to shape the world toward realizing a truly worthwhile purpose and goal. That goal has been implicit in the universe from the beginning. It would be reasonable to see it as the purpose of the cosmos in the mind of God.

•

Keith Ward is Regius Professor, Christ Church, Oxford, and former Professor of Moral Philosophy and Professor of the History and Philosophy of Religion at the University of London. He is the author of God, Chance, and Necessity *and* Defending the Soul.

After the Human Genome Project

ELVING ANDERSON

In a few years we shall have a complete map of the human genes — eighty thousand or so. The goals of the Human Genome Project will then have been met. Small sections of this genetic map have been studied already, but soon a full-scale exploration into the function of these genes will be possible. This will mark the end of the beginning and the start of the next phase of research. We embark upon it with a sense of optimism — but also fear.

New understandings will lead to new therapies that are directed at the genes themselves by enhancing the function of partially deficient genes or by reducing the expression of harmful genes. Many of the common medical problems, however, reflect the interaction of several genes with environmental factors, and their treatment will require attention to relevant aspects of lifestyle. As the eminent biologist Theodosius Dobzhansky pointed out, humans adapt their environments to their genes more often than genes adapt to environments.

But this growing understanding is also a cause for anxious concern. For example, the greatest impact may come from improved knowledge of the brain. Almost half of our genes are expressed mainly in the brain. Furthermore, the brain is complex in both structure and function, since given genes are expressed only in specific parts of the brain at certain times of life. The impact of such discoveries will become most controversial when dealing with behaviors that are distinctive features of human nature.

The prospect of such intimate self-knowledge can be exhilarating to those for whom the simple and yet complex nature of DNA inspires awe and wonder, or it can threaten the faith of those who look for the Creator's hand only in the unknown. Is it necessary to choose between genetic design and divine purpose, or between mystery and scientific explanation?

Then there is the specter of genetic determinism: the suggestion that we are merely the product of our genes. A related fear is reductionism: the idea that our lives are ultimately reducible to the action of our genes.

Several lines of evidence, however, contradict these claims. For a start, complex adaptive systems (including those formed by genes) are not fully predictable, even in principle. Identical twin pairs do not show identical behaviors. Furthermore, genes always act within a context, so that gene discovery and the development of effective treatments require careful examination of the whole individual. We can conclude that, while genes are essential for human existence and human behavior, they are by no means sufficient.

We have already come a long way in this type of research. It is sometimes difficult to realize that genetics is strictly a twentieth-century phenomenon. It was only in the early 1900s that it was realized that the genetic factors of Gregor Mendel are carried on the chromosomes. Other discoveries followed, including the recognition that mutations cause inborn errors of metabolism and that radiation causes mutations.

By midcentury we knew that DNA is the fundamental genetic material. Physical and chemical methods had revealed the basic structure and composition of the DNA. The paper by James Watson and Francis Crick resolved how genes can be copied and how information is encoded within them. More recently, a way was developed to isolate and analyze specific regions of DNA, starting even with a single cell.

It is impossible, of course, to predict what the twenty-first century will bring, but at least some of the main questions can be identified.

First, what are the functions of the genes? Present understanding of the genetic language makes it possible to sort genes into broad categories such as energy production, cell cycle control, and cell-to-cell communication. For example, we may have 50–100 genes for channels that control the flow of potassium ions across cell membranes.

Second, there is the question of how genes are regulated. Some genes are expressed in the liver, some in the heart, some in the brain, and some in all three organs. No more than 5–10 percent are used in any single cell. Many genes are turned on or off at regular times in development, while others can respond to changes in the cellular environment.

As a last point we must ask how genes interact with one another. It is now possible to analyze (on a single glass slide) the expression of thousands of DNA sequences from a specific part of the brain. How are such genes affected by environmental factors or by changes in other genes? These studies can reveal the details of complex adaptive systems based on the interaction of genes throughout life.

In the face of this growing knowledge and power we must realize that new challenges will arise in the future to test our collective humility. Experience tells us that (1) there is always more to learn (the end of the Human Genome Project is only the preparation for a new level of research), and (2) we never know enough. The results of new therapies or other forms of genetic engineering cannot be predicted accurately. We must proceed with caution, and reversibly whenever possible.

Finally, we can confidently expect that the twenty-first century will bring further evidence for an intricate genetic design that is fully consistent with belief in a Creator. In view of other interlocking complexities, however, we shall never be able adequately to describe humans solely in terms of their genes. Additional modes of understanding, including the spiritual dimension, will continue to be needed in order to complete the picture of what it is to be human.

•

Elving Anderson is Professor Emeritus of Genetics at the University of Minnesota. He is a past president of Sigma Xi, the Scientific Research Society, and other scientific societies.

All in the Genes

JOHN HABGOOD

Recent claims to have identified a gene for tallness invited the question What next? Are we to expect a constant stream of announcements as one human characteristic after another is traced back to its genetic origins, and what we think of as our humanity is revealed in all its starkness as complex chemistry? It is obvious that the enormous resources now being put into genetic research will tell us a lot more about ourselves. It is also inherent in the nature of science not to set limits on what might be discovered. But are there limits to what genetics can explain?

Genetic systems are often mistakenly described as blueprints. The essence of a blueprint is that there is a simple one-to-one relationship between what is on the plan and what is constructed from it. The discovery of genes for tallness or eye color or whatever tends to reinforce the blueprint image, but the reality is actually much less straightforward. Genes act more like bundles of instructions, setting in motion and controlling a process whose end result will depend in part on what else is happening. The fact that many of these instructions are closely linked with one another makes it extremely difficult to foretell what the result of changing any one of them is likely to be.

In more precise terms, genes manufacture proteins and enzymes, which in turn react with other proteins and enzymes to build cells, organs, and bodies. Other factors enter into this process, notably the geometrical properties of the proteins themselves, the supply of raw materials, and the environment in which it all takes place. In a tightly controlled environment, such as the uterus, and with suitable nutrition, the results are fairly predictable. But once an infant leaves the uterus, the number and variety of other influences impinging on it are huge, and all are likely to play their part in shaping the kind of person that infant will become. If genes were blueprints, fantasies about producing an identical clone of oneself would not be absurd. But because they are instructions within a process which does not depend wholly on the genes themselves, the making of identical copies is not a practical possibility. Identical twins who have shared the same environment both inside and outside the womb provide the closest approach to ideal clones, but even they frequently differ in the kind of people they are and make deliberate choices about how far they are going to emphasize their likeness.

The main interest in human genetic manipulation centers at present on the possibility of correcting defects in individual genes known to be responsible for two thousand or so serious hereditary diseases. To be lastingly effective, the corrections would have to be made at the early embryonic stage, and there are major ethical worries about permitting this degree of interference in somebody's life when there can be no certainty about what further consequences it might have.

Single defects in single genes, however, are child's play compared with the uncertainties likely to be encountered when more than one gene is involved and when complex human characteristics are the target. Claims have been made about genes for aspects of social behavior, such as aggressiveness, alcoholism, or homosexuality. But even if a genetic link is established, the effects are likely to amount to no more than a propensity to behave in certain ways, given the enormous number of other factors influencing what people do. Moreover, even if such propensities were found to be dependent on single genes, there are far too many steps, both biological and social, between a gene and a form of conduct to justify any claim that one completely determines the other.

Genetic determinism makes no sense in creatures as complex, as open to their environment, and as dependent on social interaction as human beings have always known themselves to be. But scientific talk about genes for this or that can be seductive. Unless its limitations are made clear, its tendency in the long run is to undermine moral responsibility and our sense of independent personhood. As genetic knowledge expands, and as medical techniques proliferate for manipulating or replacing some of our most vital bodily functions, the question What is a person? becomes more urgent. We need ways of understanding ourselves more comprehensively, bridging the gulfs between different academic disciplines. We need to relate the scientific story to the story of inner experience and human culture, and to acknowledge the power of language in enabling us to explore and invent other realms of being.

My conviction that this is an urgent task has been my excuse for spending a year of my retirement in writing a book which tries to link such themes with a believable theology. Our genes set the scene for what we are. They are the basis of the given reality of our bodily nature, with all its potentialities and constraints. As human beings we are unique in the degree to which these different capacities can be used in different ways. What we do with them depends to a large extent on the relationships, physical, personal, and ultimately transcendental, within which our lives develop. But from the very start our capacity for reflection, for standing back from our immediate situation, gives us the power of choice. The more we accept responsibility for what we are, the greater our freedom. To blame our genes when things go wrong is to diminish ourselves.

•

John Habgood is a former physiologist. He was ordained into the Church of England and served as Bishop of Durham and, for twelve years, as Archbishop of York. His latest book is Being a Person: Where Faith and Science Meet.

Our Genetic Future

TED PETERS

Can we use the poser of the gene to remake ourselves? Is it true that "it's all in the genes"? If so, can we get into our DNA with wrenches and screwdrivers and take control of our evolutionary future? If the genes have controlled us, can we now take control of the genes?

Everywhere we turn, we bump into the gene myth. Science is one thing. Myth is another. The myth is what we believe science tells us, whether it's true or not. The myth says, It's all in the genes! Where do we get our eye color? From the genes, of course. Where do we get our intelligence? From the genes, of course. Where do diseases such as cystic fibrosis, inherited breast cancer, and probably Alzheimer's start? In the genes, of course. So, we ask, Might everything be in the genes? How about personality traits? How about our predisposition for sinning? For loving? Where does it stop? Are we totally determined by our genes, like a puppet is totally determined by the puppeteer?

But, then, we ask, If the genes determine us, could we tell our scientist to dig into our DNA and reprogram the genes? Could we make the genes do our bidding? Could we take control of the evolutionary future of the human race? When we pursue this line of thinking, we do so as an expression of the gene myth. It's exciting. But, is it realistic? Is it ethical?

Some would say it's unethical to alter the human genetic code if it will influence persons yet to be born. They say evolution has bequeathed to us our present state of human nature, and nature knows best. If we tinker with nature, nature might take revenge on us. So, the gene myth has a moral commandment: thou shalt not play God. The commandment equates God with nature. Butter commercials used to say, "You can't fool Mother Nature." In previous decades we heard the commandment against playing God coming from the *Frankenstein* story. Now in the genetic era, it takes the form of *Jurassic Park*. In both of these stories a mad scientist invades the inner sanctum of nature, manipulates something, and then nature roars back with death and destruction. In short, the gene myth says, we ought not change the genes Mother Nature has given us.

As a theologian who has paid close attention to the frontier of genetic research, I'm impatient with the gene myth. Genes have a powerful influence on us, to be sure. But the gene myth overstates the case. It ascribes too much to genetic determinism. Genes certainly do determine eye color, and they certainly do predispose us toward certain diseases. But molecular biologists —the kind of scientists who study the chemical activities of genes—are quick to point out that it's not the genes alone. Genes interact with their environment. The gene/environment interaction is decisive, and environments vary. No one who has a genetic predisposition to alchoholism will become an alcoholic if he or she refuses to drink.

Can I freely decide to drink or not to drink? Yes. Genetic determinism does not eliminate human freedom. We are free at the complex level of the human self. To be a self is to experience freedom. We don't have to play one off against the other. We can, and do, have both genetic determinism and human freedom. We cannot decide which color of eye to be born with, to be sure. Yet we can decide when we want to put on our glasses. We know we have this freedom because we experience it every day. No amount of genetic determinism will take it away.

We also have the basic freedom to pursue a still higher freedom, namely, the good. Our genes all by themselves do not think of high-minded ideals; nor do they pursue such things as neighborly love or world peace. Only a mind does. Only a soul. Only an integrated human self dedicated to what is good can organize his or her body, including the genes, to work together to make this world a better place.

87

I agree that the commandment against playing God ought to give us pause. It ought to caution us against plunging ahead recklessly without scientific prowess. What nature has bequeathed to us in our genetic code is as complex as it is magnificent. We do not understand it all. Nor can we hope to understand it all in the near future. The risk of blunder is high. So, when tinkering with human nature, we need to do so with caution and even reverence.

Still, I don't want to shut down genetic research. The key reason is this: the future of human health is at stake. Of all human diseases, four thousand to six thousand are the result of malfunctioning genes. The scientists we affectionately call "gene hunters" are searching out those genes, looking for the switch to turn them off, and then trying to produce a pharmaceutical to govern them. Difficulties in research and potential ethical issues regarding just who will benefit abound here. Yet we must not miss the forest for the trees: genetic research is leading us to medicines and therapies that promise relief from suffering for thousands if not millions of people in the future. This is a good thing. Whether evolution put it in our DNA or not, scientific research leading to better health and diminished human suffering is a good worthy of our pursuit.

•

Ted Peters is Professor of Systematic Theology at Pacific Lutheran Theological Seminary and Graduate Theological Union in Berkeley, California. He is director of the Science and Religion Course Program at the Center for Theology and the Natural Sciences in Berkeley. Among his books is Playing God? Genetic Determinism and Human Freedom.

Genetic Engineering: Foe or Friend?

CELIA DEANE-DRUMMOND

Is genetic engineering a good or a bad thing? The new technology certainly allows vast changes in the fabric of life by altering the genes. Genes are the information blueprint that is passed on from one generation to the next. They code for particular proteins specific to the form of life. Genetic manipulation allows us to control how a species develops.

Not only that, it is now possible to move genes from one species to another, for example, from a human to a pig, or to bacteria. If we put a human gene into bacteria, they act like a factory for the human protein. This procedure is particularly effective as bacteria multiply fast compared with higher organisms, such as plants and animals. This technique involving bacteria is used in making human insulin and is of enormous benefit to those who suffer from diabetes.

Other examples of genetic modification for medical purposes include the treatment of those who suffer from genetic disease, such as cystic fibrosis.

Few of us have qualms over the use of genetic engineering for such ends. Indeed, we could celebrate this expression of our human creativity as a gift from God. Through developing ways to prevent human suffering, we become cocreators with God.

But let's consider another example. Suppose we transfer human growth hormone genes to pigs in order to make them grow quicker. If this is done, pigs soon develop arthritis, are blind, and suffer in other ways. Why? The reason is that there is no control of the human growth hormone in the pig. Unfortunately, we cannot always predict gene control after transfer to other species. Many people are worried about eating genetically modified food. The idea, for example, of eating pork that contains a human gene seems repugnant.

What about the risk to human health in eating unknown proteins in food? While the actual quantity of genetic material that we are likely to take in is small, we still feel uneasy. We might also worry about unknown allergic reactions of all kinds. Are we somehow "playing God" in moving genes across species? In the Genesis story God declares that the natural order is "good." For some religious believers the idea of any interference with the order in the natural world seems like human arrogance.

But in order to assess this we need to think about the extent to which the natural world is "untouchable." Human beings have helped to change the natural world since the dawn of human existence. All through history we have cultivated crops, domesticated animals, and so forth. While Christians insist on respect for the natural world, they reject any idea that creation is divine. However, all creatures are gifts from God that deserve respect. So in assessing a particular proposal we need to ask, Does this show sufficient respect for the creature? We also need to ask whether we can justify the action. Changing bacteria or plants raises different questions compared with changing animals or humans. Is the particular change allowable, and if so, does the potential benefit outweigh the risk?

I suggest that the particular quality we need now is wisdom—wisdom to discern our motives. We also need to ask if our ingenuity has outstripped our wisdom.

All great religions have given us a source of wisdom through many centuries. Our desire for knowledge has often blinded us to the need to develop wisdom. In fixing on a certain goal we fail to look at the whole picture. By wisdom I mean the ability to have the widest possible perspective on life, to see things as a whole. It includes reason but recognizes that reason is only part of the story.

A theological approach to wisdom becomes the quest for goodness and truth. Our conduct, then, is judged by the goodness it promotes for the whole global community. We need this breadth if we are going to allow for views different than our own. Early scientists were well aware of the need to combine their research with their religious insights. Their desire was to work for the common good. Isaac Newton, the founder of modern physics, spent as much time in the study of theology as of physics. The split between science and religion is a relatively modern occurrence over the past few hundred years.

There are those who object to genetic engineering because of the environmental risks. Genetix Snowball is a protest group that has acted directly to "decontaminate" fields of genetically modified crops. The risk in most cases is actually far less than the group suggests. Yet it does stir up fear in the minds of most ordinary people. Such outbursts reinforce the idea that the changes are too rapid for most people to handle psychologically. Some of the fears are genuine and need to be listened to carefully.

Again, we need to reflect on the wisdom of certain developments. Questions such as, Will it make a profit? or Will it increase efficiency? should be be asked alongside What are the social consequences? and Is this a wise move in view of the unknown risks?

All of this suggests that while there are obviously huge benefits to be gained from genetic engineering, there are always some risks. But I wonder how many of us would object to genetic engineering if it produced a lifesaving drug for one of our children? These are complex issues that require more thought, more collaboration on everyone's part.

•

Celia Deane-Drummond is Senior Lecturer in Applied Theology at University College in Chester, UK. Following upon her doctorate in plant physiology, and ten years' research and lecturing in plant science, she took a doctorate in theology. Deane-Drummond's more recent books include A Handbook in Theology and Ecology *and* Theology and Biotechnology: Implications for a New Science.

Cloning: Promise of Immortality – or Threat?

MICHAEL NORTHCOTT

Eight clinics in the Far East, North America, and the United Kingdom are in a race to produce cloned human embryos. The technique used in cloning, known as nuclear transfer, was first developed by the Scottish scientist Ian Wilmut in the production of Dolly the sheep. DNA is transferred into an embryo through a needle thinner than a human hair, and successfully fertilized embryos may then be transferred into the womb. The technique is unreliable and for every regenerated embryo, hundreds are not viable. But a small number of cloned sheep, and many hundreds of cloned mice, have already been born, and viable cloned embryos, using human DNA and the outer "sac" of an embryo taken from a cow, have been produced in a laboratory in Massachusetts.

When it was first developed, most scientists said that nuclear transfer technology should not be used for human cloning. Now Wilmut, and many of his colleagues in the cloning race, support human cloning. Some, including Wilmut, want to limit the technique to medical cloning. The idea is that couples with a history of serious genetic disorders, such as cystic fibrosis, submit their sperm and embryos to test-tube embryo fertilization. Scientists would take a successfully fertilized embryo, remove the defective gene which causes the condition, and clone the genetically cleaned-up embryo. The cloned embryo would then be implanted in the mother, who would give birth to a cloned child which in every respect, but for the disease-inducing gene, would be identical to her original embryo.

Some scientists want to use cloning to treat not just medical genetic disorders but also reproductive disorders in couples for whom conventional fertility treatments are unsuccessful. Some are even prepared to help individuals have children who will be exact genetic copies of themselves. Wealthy individuals in the United States, the Middle East, and the

Far East are already putting up big money to laboratories in the hope that they will be able to clone themselves.

Human cloning would in theory allow the engineering of test-tube babies whose genetic inheritance would be unparalleled in the history of human evolution. Propensities to diseases with a known genetic component such as heart disease could be removed. At the same time, scientists could genetically enhance physical and even mental characteristics such as intelligence, eyesight, and height. Even personality traits, such as a propensity to addictive behavior, could in theory be corrected. The result would be the creation of "designer babies," and ultimately of a new race of genetically superior humans. In the high-tech labs of the bioengineers the twentieth-century idea of eugenics, which came closest to reality in the racial engineering and genocide of Adolf Hitler's evil Third Reich, may finally be realized. Instead of a master race, the new eugenics could produce a superclass of genetically enhanced human beings whose superiority would be designed by scientists and parents wealthy enough to pay for the technology to clone themselves, their embryos, or their children.

The declared intention of promoters of the new eugenics is to improve the human condition and reduce suffering and disease. But what kind of society will this new eugenics create, and is it one we would want ourselves and our children to live in? In Aldous Huxley's Brave New World, and in the futuristic film Gattaca, genetically engineered societies are dark and threatening places in which the genetic underclass—or "degenerates"—are virtual slaves to the genetically enhanced super race. Critics of genetic engineering, such as Jeremy Rifkin, author of The Biotech Century, believe that human cloning will change the meaning of human identity and reproduction, and even alter the course of evolution.

93

Rifkin fears that by playing with the blueprint of human life, scientists, with possibly disastrous consequences, will be able to control how individuals, and ultimately the human species, are brought into the world.

Throughout their history, Christians have witnessed to a uniquely material and bodily vision of salvation from human failings, and from disease and death, a vision which they find revealed in the life, death, and resurrection of Jesus of Nazareth. For most of the first two millennia of the Christian Era, Christians saw life in the body as a preparation for a good death. They saw physical death as a transformation of identity— both body and soul—into a life of intimate union and joyful praise of God which is made possible in the resurrection of Jesus who is "the first born of the dead."

The scientific quest for genetically engineered human perfection, and for deferred death through cloned organ transplants, is a manifestation of the modern fear of death in a society in which belief in resurrection is no longer widely shared. But the irony is that as we devote our best minds and considerable resources to extending the physical limits of human existence for the privileged few, the lives of millions are being blighted by environmental catastrophe. The values, wealth, and technology which are bringing about the new eugenics are the same as those which are placing such severe strain on the physical limits of the life-support systems of the planet.

Many who no longer practice Christianity, and even some who do, increasingly substitute belief in reincarnation for belief in resurrection. But whichever we believe, both doctrines involve the idea that our personal identity and our present bodily existence are not identical. Both acknowledge limits to bodily existence. And both indicate that human happiness is to be found not by denying these limits but by acknowledging

94

them, and by restraining obsessive desires for material wealth or bodily perfection, and even longevity. Resisting these limits in a quest for wealth and technologies which together can create new cloned children, or even cloned organs, will not save us or our children from death. But owning that there are limits to what we should do with technology just might help to save the planet, as well as our genetic inheritance, in their flawed but still wondrous diversity, for our children and our children's children.

•

Michael Northcott is Lecturer in Christian Ethics and in the Sociology of Religion at the University of Edinburgh and is ordained in the Church of England. His books include The Environment and Christian Ethics *and* Life after Debt: Christianity and Global Justice.

Part Six

Faith, Medicine, and Well-being

In the developed countries of the world we have grown accustomed to an ever increasing standard of living. The lure of accumulated riches has long held out the prospect of happiness. **David Myers** summarizes the latest research demonstrating the illusory nature of this promise.

A sense of well-being can be dependent on one's state of health. A notable field of research that has opened up in recent years is the scientific study of the health benefits associated with religious observance—what has come to be known in medical circles as "the forgotten factor." **Dale Matthews** points out that there are now more than three hundred studies conclusively demonstrating the medical value of religious commitment. In the light of this evidence, physicians would do well to encourage patients to continue with, or at least consider, authentic religious activity.

It has been demonstrated that those who go to church on a regular basis live longer, on average, than those who do not. As **Harold Koenig** puts it, not going to church has the equivalent effect on mortality of smoking one pack of cigarettes per day for forty years. In addition to physical benefits, religion has been demonstrated to be particularly helpful in regard to mental health. Of course, it remains to be seen whether the association between religion and good health is a causal one. But either way, the effects cannot be ignored.

The healing power of holding to a faith in an Infinite Absolute is so pronounced that **Herbert Benson** and **Patricia Myers** are led to wonder whether such faith could have become incorporated by natural selection in our genes. If this is the case, it would still remain an open question whether such a gene was implanted by a God who intended us to seek after the divine.

Wealth and Well-being

DAVID MYERS

Does money buy happiness? Few of us would agree that it does. But would a little more money make us a little happier? Many of us smirk and nod. There is, we believe, some connection between wealth and well-being, between fiscal fitness and emotional fulfillment. Most of us tell Gallup that, yes, we would like to be rich. Three in four entering American collegians—nearly double the 1970 proportion—now consider it "very important" or "essential" that they become "very well off financially." Money matters.

Think of it as today's American dream: life, liberty, and the purchase of happiness. "*Of course* money buys happiness," writes Andrew Tobias. Wouldn't anyone be happier with the indulgences promised by the magazine sweepstakes: a forty-foot yacht, deluxe motor home, private housekeeper? "Whoever said money can't buy happiness isn't spending it right," proclaimed a Lexus ad.

Well, *are* rich people happier? Researchers have found that in poor countries, such as Bangladesh and India, being relatively well off does make for somewhat greater well-being. Psychologically as well as materially, it is better not to be desperately poor. We *need* food, rest, shelter, social contact.

But in countries where nearly everyone can afford life's necessities, increasing affluence matters surprisingly little. The correlation between income and happiness is "surprisingly weak," as the University of Michigan researcher Ronald Inglehart observed in a sixteen-nation study of 170,000 people. Once a person is comfortable, more money provides diminishing returns. The second piece of pie, or the second $100,000, never tastes as good as the first.

Even very rich people—including the Forbes's one hundred wealthiest Americans surveyed by the University of Illinois psychologist Ed Diener—are only slightly happier than the average American. Those whose income has increased over a ten-year period are not happier than those on stable incomes. And lottery winners typically gain but a temporary jolt of joy. Wealth, it seems, is like health: although its utter absence can breed misery, possessing it fails to guarantee happiness. Happiness seems less a matter of getting what we want than of wanting what we have.

We can also ask whether, over time, our collective happiness has floated upward with the rising economic tide. Are we happier today than in 1940, when two out of five homes lacked a shower or tub, heat often meant feeding wood or coal into a furnace, and 35 percent of homes had no toilet? Or consider 1957, when economist John Kenneth Galbraith was about to describe the United States as the affluent society. Americans' per person income, expressed in today's dollars, was $8,700. Today it is $20,000. Compared to 1957, we are now "the doubly affluent society"—with double what money buys. We have twice as many cars per person. We eat out two and a half times as often. And, compared to the late 1950s, when few Americans had dishwashers, clothes dryers, or air conditioning, most do today.

So, believing that a little more money would make us a little happier and that it's important to be very well off, are we in fact—after four decades of gradually rising affluence—now happier?

We are not. Since 1957, the number of Americans telling the University of Chicago's National Opinion Research Center that they are "very happy" has declined from 35 to 30 percent. Meanwhile, the divorce rate has doubled, the teen suicide rate has tripled, the violent crime rate has quadrupled, and rates of depression have mushroomed, especially among teens and younger adults. These are the best of times materially, "a time of elephantine vanity and greed," observed Garrison Keillor. But they are not the best of times for the human spirit. Our becoming much better off over the past four decades has not been accompanied by one iota of increased psychological well-being.

The same is true of the European countries and Japan. In Britain, for example, sharp increases in the percentage of households with cars, central heating, and telephones have not been accompanied by increased happiness. This fact of life explodes a bombshell underneath our society's materialism: *economic growth in affluent countries has provided no boost to human morale.* When it comes to psychological well-being, it is not "the economy, stupid."

We know it, sort of. In a nationally representative survey, the Princeton sociologist Robert Wuthnow found that 89 percent of people felt "our society is much too materialistic." *Other* people are too materialistic, that is. For 84 percent also wished they had more money, and 78 percent said it was "very or fairly important" to have "a beautiful home, a new car and other nice things."

But one has to wonder, what's the point? "Why," asked the prophet Isaiah, "do you spend your money for that which is not bread, and your labor for that which does not satisfy?" What's the point of accumulating stacks of unplayed CDs, closets full of seldom-worn clothes, garages with luxury cars—all purchased in a vain quest for an elusive joy?

A *Newsweek* cover story on Ted Turner's billion-dollar pledge to the United Nations reported that "eighty percent of all estates of more than $1 million leave *nothing* to charity." But again, one has to wonder: what's the point of leaving huge estates for one's heirs, as if inherited wealth could buy them happiness, when that wealth could do so much good in a hurting world?

Ted Turner, give him credit, seems to understand the modest connection between wealth and well-being, and he seems to have found liberation from envying those who have more. So have at least a few other billionaires, such as George Soros and John Templeton. Perhaps their example can inspire their peers, and all of us, to an alms race—or at least to rethink our stewardship of wealth.

•

David Myers is Professor of Psychology at Hope College in Holland, Michigan, and is the author of psychology's most studied textbook. Among his recent books are From Chaos to Community: America's Social Recession and Renewal *and* The Pursuit of Happiness: Who Is Happy—and Why.

Is Religion Good for Your Health?

DALE MATTHEWS

Is religion good for your health? Do prayer and faith have a prayer of helping you heal?

A vivacious—and vexing—lady visited my medical office often, armed with a beguiling smile, a rapier wit, and intractable pain from arthritis. Each visit brought forth a languorous litany of incurable woe: she had sampled every painkiller in the pharmacopoeia, with scant success.

"Is there anything that does help you?" I asked one day, in desperation.

"Faith and prayer!" she exclaimed. "And singing in the church choir!"

Faith, prayer . . . and singing? Are these listed in the *Physician's Desk Reference?* Should they be? Karl Marx dismissed religion as "the opiate of the people." Is religion, like codeine and other opiates, an effective "drug" for pain and other disorders? What's the proper dose? Are there side effects?

The medical effects of faith are a matter not just of faith but also of science. More than three hundred scientific studies demonstrate the medical value of religious commitment (including worship attendance, prayer, Scripture study, and active participation in a spiritual community). These benefits include enhanced prevention and treatment of mental disorders (e.g., depression, suicide, and anxiety), medical and surgical illnesses (e.g., heart disease, cancer, sexually transmitted diseases), and addictions; reduced pain and disability; and prolonged survival. In addition, spiritual treatment (e.g., prayer, religiously based psychotherapy) enhances recovery.

For the faithful, religious commitment offers many health advantages. A cohesive, comforting set of beliefs and participation in sacred rituals may endow a sense of meaning, purpose, and hope. Faith offers a "peace that passeth understanding" in times of pain, grief, and disability. Healthy lifestyle choices (e.g., exercise, proper diet) are more common and unhealthy behaviors (e.g., nicotine, alcohol, and drug use; suicide attempts; high-risk sexual activity) less common among religious persons. Persons of faith usually cope effectively with stress and have strong social support and a high quality of life (e.g., well-being, self-esteem, job and marital satisfaction, altruism).

In this health-conscious age, patients are demanding more from medical professionals. They want more compassion and less dispassion, more listening and less lecturing; they seek healers of the mind and spirit, not just mechanics of the body. According to recent scientific studies and polls, two out of three individuals would like to address spiritual issues with their doctors, and half would even like their doctors to pray with them.

Is this something new? The latest fad? Actually, the bond between religion and medicine is quite ancient. Since the dawn of recorded history, these twin traditions of healing have been partners in the care of the sick, plowing together the holy ground of healing.

The success of modern medical practice came at a price: there seemed to be "no room at the inn" for religion in healing. Nonetheless, the dogged persistence of chronic diseases and the alarming advances of AIDS and other scourges have tempered any hope or expectation that science will eventually, inevitably solve all mysteries of illness.

A new willingness to consider alternative healing practices and a growing civility between religion and medicine is in the air. It's time to reunite these long-separated twin traditions of healing; to join hands, not swords.

In my office, I encourage everyone to exercise regularly, eat properly, cease smoking and excessive alcohol use, take medicines correctly, and even wear seatbelts. Should I tell them to pray, read Scripture, attend worship, or work at a soup kitchen?

My answer is yes! The documented health benefits of religious beliefs and practices and the burgeoning spiritual interests of patients compel us to address matters of faith with our patients. All medical professionals can learn to recognize the medical impact of faith and to encourage, when appropriate, the healthy use of spiritual beliefs and practices. Praying for or with patients may be a valuable, meaningful option in certain instances, depending on the beliefs and wishes of both the patient and the doctor.

Some cautions are in order regarding possible "side effects." While some clinicians may develop particular expertise in handling spiritual problems, physicians will not replace clergy: each role is unique, and both are needed in the care of the sick. Similarly, I do not suggest or sanction use of faith-based approaches *instead of* medical care: we need prayer and Prozac, clergy and clinicians, faith and medicine.

Participating in prayer and religious activities does not guarantee good health: both saints and sinners alike eventually get sick and die. Patients should not follow "doctor's orders" in matters of faith: choosing a particular spiritual tradition (or none at all) should not be forced, nor should it be based on the mistaken belief that one faith offers a greater likelihood of obtaining health benefits than another. Indeed, the very purpose of faith is not merely to lower blood pressure or add a few moments or months of life, but to seek truth and find God.

Despite these legitimate concerns, I do believe that physicians can —and should—encourage patients to continue or consider authentic, autonomous religious activity. Perhaps clinicians of the twenty-first century will join with clergy to develop a new synthesis of scientifically based and religiously meaningful medical care to help persons who suffer and seek our aid.

Shall we pray?

•

Dale Matthews is Associate Professor of Medicine at the Georgetown University School of Medicine in Washington, D.C., and a Fellow of the American College of Physicians. He is the author of a four-volume work titled The Faith Factor: An Annotated Bibliography of Clinical Research on Spiritual Subjects.

The Healing Power of Faith

HAROLD KOENIG

Religion is widespread and deeply influences our society, culture, and health practices. Recent Gallup surveys indicate that 96 percent of Americans believe in God or a universal spirit, 90 percent pray, and 43 percent attend church weekly or more often. Only within the past few years, however, has it been more generally known that religious beliefs and practices have an impact on physical and mental health.

Religion is commonly relied upon to cope with the stress caused by health problems. Systematic research indicates that in some parts of the United States, 90 percent of persons with serious medical illness use religion at least to some degree as a coping resource, and approximately 50 percent of those persons report that religious faith is the most important factor that enables them to cope (i.e., it is more important than family, friends, work, or any other known coping resources).

Medical science is now beginning to substantiate this claim. At least four studies in the 1990s have been published in the *American Journal of Psychiatry* demonstrating that religious persons are less likely to become depressed, and if they do experience depression, are more likely to recover quicker from this disorder. Religious beliefs provide a worldview that gives meaning and purpose to life, helps make sense of tragedy and suffering, and often enables people to transcend even the most difficult of circumstances. It is not surprising, then, that studies are increasingly showing that religious persons experience greater well-being, higher life satisfaction, and less anxiety; abuse alcohol and drugs less often; and are much less likely to commit suicide.

These mental health benefits of religious faith have physical health consequences. Mind/body medicine is one of the fastest-growing areas of medical science, as investigators throughout the world have turned their attention to the effects of mental stress, emotional disorder, and social isolation on the human body. When persons experience stress, are socially marginalized, or become depressed, there are physiological processes that if allowed to continue over time result in blood pressure elevation, heart attacks, stroke, stomach ulcers, irritable bowel, and impaired immune function (increasing the risk of infection and possibly cancer). Thus, any resource that helps reduce stress, relieve depression, or increase social support will help reduce or prevent these negative health consequences.

Among the most powerful of such resources is religion. Religion not only helps people cope better with stress because of comforting beliefs, it also increases social contacts and leads to the development of mutually supportive relationships. Religious marriages tend to last longer, be more fulfilling, and end in divorce less often, thus providing more stable environments in which health issues are tended to. Such supportive relationships often increase the likelihood that diseases will be detected early and that medical treatments will be complied with. For example, church members tend to check up on each other, particularly if someone is having health problems or does not show up at church on Sunday.

Active religious involvement also improves health by its effects on health behaviors. Religious persons are less likely to smoke cigarettes, abuse alcohol or drugs, or engage in risky sexual practices. Because religious persons tend to have stable marriages, children raised in religious homes are less likely to abuse alcohol and drugs, less likely to commit criminal or delinquent activities, and less likely to engage in promiscuous sexual activity—all of which will likely affect health later in life.

It is not surprising, then, that three major studies (recently published in the *American Journal of Public Health* and the *Journal of Gerontology*) performed in different parts of the United States by different research teams have found religiously active people living considerably longer than the nonreligious. The lack of religious involvement has an effect on mortality that is equivalent to forty years of smoking one pack of cigarettes per day.

Several studies have now discovered a connection between religious involvement and immune system function. For example, in a study of 1,718 subjects age sixty-five or over conducted by Duke University researchers, low levels of church attendance were associated with higher levels of interleukin-6 (IL 6), a blood protein indicative of immune system dysfunction. Higher levels of religious attendance in 1986, 1989, and 1992 all predicted lower IL-6 levels in 1992. High levels of IL-6 ($<$ 5 ng/ml) are found in persons with AIDS, osteoporosis, Alzheimer's disease, diabetes, and certain forms of cancer. Frequent church attenders were only half as likely as nonattenders to have high levels of IL-6 in their blood, suggesting that they have stronger immune systems. Likewise, studies of patients with AIDS indicate stronger immune system functioning among those who are more religiously involved. Thus there are many mechanisms by which religion may both extend the length of life and enhance its quality and meaning.

While the effects of religion on mental and physical health are in general positive, they can be negative as well. Occasionally one will encounter small, often fringe, religious groups which avoid contact with health professionals. Such groups may on religious grounds encourage members to stop lifesaving medications, avoid medical professionals, fail to vaccinate their children, not seek prenatal care, or reject other medical treatments. Studies of these groups show shortened survival and increased mortality.

Likewise, some religious beliefs are repressive and controlling, rather than guiding and liberating. Religion may instill fear, foster obsessive-compulsive traits, and lead to closed-mindedness and prejudice. The Jonestown, Guyana mass suicide and the Waco, Texas Branch Davidian tragedy are disturbing reminders of the fact that religion can have negative health effects. The scientific evidence for religion's negative effects on health, however, is far less compelling than the mounting research that shows positive effects.

•

Harold Koenig is Associate Professor of Psychiatry and founder-director of the Center for the Study of Religion/Spirituality and Health at Duke University in Durham, North Carolina. Among his eleven books is The Healing Power of Faith.

Medical Aspects of Belief

HERBERT BENSON AND
PATRICIA MYERS

An extensive literature reveals that religious commitment is associated with increased survival; reduced alcohol, cigarette, and drug use; reduced anxiety, depression, and anger; reduced blood pressure; and improved quality of life for patients with cancer and heart disease. In addition, religious people consistently report greater life satisfaction, marital satisfaction, well-being, altruism, and self-esteem than do nonreligious people.

Belief in God lends us a will to live that we would not have without God. This may be why religion becomes more important to us as we age. As we draw closer to the inevitable onset of declining health and death, the torment grows and our need to venerate our current experience expands proportionally. This is why people in the midst of life-threatening disease find solace in religion, why congregations pray for those who are hospitalized, and why some Catholics want priests to read the last rites.

Faith in an invincible, infallible force carries a remarkable healing power. Believing in an Infinite Absolute appears to be part of our nature. One can reason that by the process of natural selection, mutating genes have deemed faith important for the survival of our forebears. Ironically, then, it can be argued that evolution favors religion, causing our brains to generate the impulses we need to carry on; faith, hope, and love have become part of the way humans approach living.

As long as people have lived, they have worshiped. And as Karen Armstrong writes in *A History of God*, "Jews, Christians, and Muslims have developed remarkably similar ideas of God, which also resemble other contemplations of the Absolute. When people try to find an ultimate meaning and value in human life, their minds seem to go in a certain direction. They have not been coerced to do this; it is something that seems natural to humanity." Indeed, a belief in God is natural to humanity, as natural as our instincts to fight or flee. These predetermined instincts often result in the formation of common archetypes, with common fears and tendencies becoming legends in every culture. Similarly, we develop ideas of the Almighty because we seem to be programmed to "go in a certain direction."

However, as the author Kathryn Harrison puts it, "The modern world's replacement of faith with science means that, for most of us, there is no Mystery, only mysteries, and that . . . we are about to solve [them]." Our society subjects everything to empirical analysis, in an attempt to reduce the number of unknowns and eventually reduce our understanding of the whole world to columns of statistics and formulas. And, perhaps in this way, it tries to tame the wildest variables—destiny, human choices, interpersonal relationships, and all other mysteries—and make them succinct and predictable.

Yet, even when we acquire new information, even when we have solved mysteries, we feel vaguely empty and unfulfilled, and faith becomes our long-term solace. In part, this occurs because faith in an Infinite Absolute is an adequate counterforce to the inevitability of disease and death. But it is also because faith allows us to appreciate the unseen and unproved, generating a kind of hope that cannot be secured by reason. Armstrong writes that primitive men and women worshiped gods "not simply because they wanted to propitiate powerful forces; these early faiths expressed the wonder and mystery that seem always to have been an essential part of the human experience of this beautiful yet terrifying world."

Spiritual beliefs quiet the mind, short-circuiting the unproductive reasoning that so often consumes our thoughts. The body is very effective at healing itself, but all too often this process is hindered by negative thoughts and doubts. Worries and doubts elicit the fight-or-flight response and its attendant stress-related symptoms and disease which can blunt evolutionarily honed healing capacities. Moreover, perpetual worries and doubts literally make an impression on our nerve cells, so the body tends to "remember" illness.

But because faith seems to transcend experience, it is supremely good at relieving distress and generating hope and expectancy. With hope and expectancy comes "remembered wellness"—the cerebral message for healing that mobilizes the body's resources and reactions. Remembered wellness encompasses three sets of belief: belief of the patient; belief of the healthcare provider; and belief engendered by the relationship between the patient and the healthcare provider. Such beliefs are effective in treating 50 to 90 percent of the most common medical problems. Unfortunately, medicine has frequently ridiculed this phenomenon, labeling it the placebo effect.

Some contend that humans invented the idea of God over time as a crutch or balm to stave off an otherwise cruel reality of pointlessness. And yet others maintain that the capacity for faith and for conjuring up God—what many would call the "soul"—was genetically implanted by a divine Maker who wanted to be known to us. Do we have faith because God intended us to worship, pray, yearn, and be fulfilled by believing in an Infinite Absolute? It is impossible for science to determine which came first: human beings or God.

From the very narrow perspective of healing and medicine, it does not matter which came first. Affirmative beliefs and hopes are therapeutic, and faith in God, in particular, has many positive effects on health. There are, of course, many other beneficial aspects of belief in God beyond that of medicine and healing. We honor and respect these features, and they clearly transcend the focus of this discussion.

•

Herbert Benson is founding president of the Mind/Body Medical Institute in Boston, Massachusetts, and Associate Professor of Medicine at Harvard Medical School.

Patricia Myers is Research Associate at the Mind/Body Medical Institute.

Part Seven

The Mind

It is commonly thought that psychological studies are inherently hostile to religious belief. This perception stems largely from the dominant role of Sigmund Freud, an avowed atheist, in the early development of psychoanalysis. As **Dan Blazer** explains, Freud originally tried to reduce people to hydraulics, likening the mind to a steam engine with pressures contained by valves. Later he came to accept that neurotic conflicts cannot be reduced to molecules and brain chemistry—he had to engage in "soul talk."

Today among certain biologists there is once more a drive to try to answer life's ultimate questions solely in terms of the physical. Care of the psyche, for example, is just care of the brain. But psychiatrists find—as Freud did before them—that this simply does not work. Some are expressing renewed interest in the spiritual and seek dialogue with theologians of all faith traditions.

What can brain science say about religious experience? **Fraser Watts** points out that there is a wide variety of experiences that are perceived to be "religious." Indeed, to the believer, the whole of life is permeated with the sense of the religious. That being so, it is unlikely that scientists will be able to locate a unique "God spot" in the brain. But even if they did, there would be no reason for concluding that God was not being genuinely revealed through such experiences.

In the Eastern tradition, there has always been a close link between the spiritual and art. **Vilayanur Ramachandran,** who is both a Hindu and a neuroscientist, describes how an explanation of art appreciation in terms of our evolutionary roots need not detract from the transcendent quality of art.

Freud Works with God? Unlikely Allies

Can the disciples of Sigmund Freud and the religious possibly become allies? This idea is not as strange as it sounds. Many psychiatrists today are concerned about the loss of the soul of their profession. By "soul" I mean life experiences from the viewpoint of the person and the recognition of those experiences by the psychiatrist. The pace of psychiatric practice has increased with managed care. Patients are fit into the Procrustean bed of a diagnosis based on the most recent edition of *The Diagnostic and Statistical Manual of Mental Disorders*. Treatments prescribed are frequently cookbook, with a pharmacologic recipe for virtually every problem. The critique of modern psychiatry has come most vocally from the Freudian or psychoanalytic tradition. Psychiatrists, they say, need to listen more and medicate less. Psychoanalysts are even expressing an interest in the spiritual! What is happening to the age-old debate between Freud and God?

Freud was an avowed atheist. He originally tried to reduce people to hydraulics, suggesting that our minds and emotions are like steam engines, with pressures (drives) being contained by valves (repression) and escaping in unnatural ways (neuroses). The sexual drive is the primary energy for this machine. God is manufactured in the minds of people to contain and control this excess energy. If God could be eliminated, that energy could be better channeled through mature sexual expression, among other behaviors. Freud modified his early theories, but he never gave up on a biological basis for understanding and treating emotional suffering. Yet he recognized that theory was one thing, practice another.

Freud learned early in his career that he could not view the workings of this machine directly. He listened to people, to their hopes, their fears, their dreams, and their beliefs. He helped his patients to understand

themselves and held to the end of his career that self- understanding was
the means to emotional well-being. Freud never gave up his belief that
body and soul were one. Yet to ease emotional pain, he spoke to the soul,
not the body of the person. Freud became a soul doctor, for he was intrigued by the soul and its expression in society as well as in therapy.
He explored culture and religion extensively during the latter years of his
career and even pursued a friendly correspondence with a Presbyterian
minister, Oscar Pfister. Freud might be considered a nonreductive phys-
icalist. He believed that body and soul were one, and the one was physical. Nevertheless, he could not reduce neurotic conflicts to molecules
and brain chemistry, either in his theory or in his practice. He could only
engage in "soul talk."

The 1990s were labeled the Decade of the Brain by the National Institute of Mental Health in the United States. Psychiatry has benefited
greatly from a better understanding of how the brain works. Severe depression, for example, is conceived as an abnormality of genes and molecules. The treatment, therefore, changes abnormal biological function
to normal function. Our knowledge of the brain has led to the development of designer drugs for depression that are more effective, and
produce fewer side effects, than the drugs available a decade ago. Psychiatry has therefore followed the reductionistic approach to emotional
well-being so well described by Edward O. Wilson in his recent book
Consilience. Wilson attempts to capture the entire human experience,
from health to the humanities, in one grand scheme. That scheme is
grounded in biology. So far, Wilson and Freud sound similar. Yet Wilson
proposes that the answers to life's ultimate questions are best sought
through an understanding of biology. For psychiatrists, this means that

the care of the psyche is the care of the brain. If we know the brain, we will know the soul.

Psychiatrists, however, are finding that reducing an experience such as severe depression to biology just does not work. Though medications may relieve symptoms, they fall far short of healing the emotions and comforting the soul. While finding the brain, psychiatry has perhaps lost its soul. For this reason, persons who formally sought psychiatric treatment are looking elsewhere. Some look to religion, some to New Age experiences, some to soul searching through the plethora of books now available. Thomas Moore's *Care of the Soul* reached number one on the *New York Times* best-seller list. People are searching their souls and seeking meaningful spiritual experiences, and psychiatrists are taking note.

For many years, psychiatry was viewed by religious persons as the enemy. That view was based in large part on the public's perception of Freud. These views, by the way, were not always accurate. Many Freudians (that is, the psychoanalysts) today are expressing a renewed interest in the spiritual and seeking a dialogue with theologians of all faith traditions. One bridge between these unlikely allies is narrative, the story of emotional suffering. Psychiatrists realize that our stories cannot be told without reference to spiritual struggles and spiritual highs within a faith tradition. Theologians realize that we may best understand our faith through stories, our individual stories interwoven into the stories of our faith traditions. For example, our struggle for freedom may be interwoven with the story of the exodus from Egypt by the Hebrews. Rather than challenging the faith of their patients, psychiatrists call upon the strength of their patients' faith.

Would Freud turn over in his grave if he knew of this alliance? Maybe, but I don't think so.

•

Daniel Blazer is Distinguished Professor of Psychiatry and Behavioral Sciences at Duke University School of Medicine in Durham, North Carolina, and past president of the Psychiatric Research Society. He has been a recipient of the Senior Investigator Award from the American Geriatric Society and the Distinguished Service Award from the University of North Carolina School of Public Health. Among his twenty published books is Freud versus God: How Psychiatry Lost its Soul and Christianity Lost its Mind.

Brain Science and Religious Experience

FRASER WATTS

Have you ever had a religious experience? If so, what do you think was going on in your brain at the time? If scientists could tell us what brain processes are involved in religious experience, would that mean that the experience wasn't valid? Many people seem to think that knowing what brain processes are involved will show that religious experiences are simply thrown up by neurons in the brain. But it won't show that at all.

The brain is involved in every experience we have, for example, when scientists are making discoveries. But the scientific discoveries are no less valid for knowing what went on in the brains of the scientists who made them. But, you might say, isn't religion different? We usually assume that religious experiences come from outside ourselves, from God. Couldn't they just be thrown up by the brain instead? Yes, they could be—but not necessarily. Knowing how the brain is involved in religious experience doesn't settle things one way or the other.

But shouldn't we always go for the simplest explanation when we can? If you can explain religious experience just in terms of brain processes, isn't that better than invoking God? Again, not necessarily. In physics, the elegant, simple theory often turns out to be right. Not with human beings. We are so complex that simple theories about us usually turn out to be wrong. If the truth is complex, you need a complex theory.

Is there any reason at all to think that God might be behind religious experience? The rational attraction of belief in God is that it makes plausible sense of a broad range of different things. It offers a single unifying explanation for, say, the astonishing fruitfulness of the universe, the claims of religious leaders like Jesus, and for powerful religious experiences. That isn't a knockdown argument, but it is at least a rational way of looking at things.

The current favorite theory of the role of the brain in religious experience links it with epilepsy. Some people have claimed that the part of the "temporal lobes" responsible for epilepsy is also the "God spot." It is a fashionable theory, but the evidence for it is weak.

One claim is that religious experiences are rather like epileptic seizure experiences. Yes, there are some similarities, such as the idea that the everyday world is not quite "real." However, there are also big differences. For example, seizure experiences are generally slightly alarming, whereas religious experiences bring a sense of tranquillity and purpose that often stays with people for life. The other pillar of the epilepsy theory is that people who suffer from epilepsy are supposed to be unusually mystical. It once looked as though that was true, but more careful research hasn't supported it.

Despite the lack of evidence for it, the epilepsy theory is slow to die. It has came up again in a new book, *Phantoms of the Brain*, by the American brain scientist, V. S. Ramachandran. It caught the headlines, but his only new evidence is that two patients who had both epilepsy and religious preoccupations showed strong physiological responses to religious words. That finding doesn't prove anything.

The epilepsy theory of religious experience looks like being a false trail. At best, it will be just a part of a much bigger theory. However, the problems of this one particular theory don't mean that we won't get a better one.

Another theory has been developed by a brain scientist in Pennsylvania, Eugene D'Aquili, who died recently. He was not looking for a single God spot in the brain. He thought that different parts of the brain are involved in different aspects of religion. For example, one part of the brain is involved in the sense of "unity" that is common in religious experience. A different one is involved in seeing God at work in the world.

Religious experiences are very different from one another. Some are striking, memorable experiences that stay with people for life. Recent surveys show that about a third of the population have that kind of religious experience. However, a lot of "religious" experiences are much more mundane. In fact, we can experience anything at all in a religious way. In that sense, all the experiences of a deeply religious person would be religious experiences. The fact that religious experiences are so different from one another means that the brain processes involved will be very different. No simple theory of a God spot in the brain can be adequate.

D'Aquili's theory is different from the epilepsy theory in another way. He thinks that the parts of the brain involved in religion are also involved in normal processes. For example, he suggests that seeing that one thing is caused by another depends on the same part of the brain as seeing God at work in the world. That is very different from saying that religion arises from the same kind of malfunctioning of the brain as epilepsy.

How the brain is involved in religion is a topic at the frontiers of science. It is linked to the problem of how the brain gives rise to any kind of consciousness, which is perhaps one of the biggest mysteries left for science to solve. Progress with that general problem will help us to understand how the brain is involved in religious experience.

●

Fraser Watts is Starbridge Lecturer in Theology and Natural Science at the University of Cambridge; he is a past president of the British Psychological Society and a former research psychologist at the Medical Research Council's Applied Psychology Unit. Watts is an ordained minister of the Church of England.

The Science of Art

VILAYANUR RAMACHANDRAN

What is art? In the Eastern tradition, special emphasis is laid on the link between art and the spiritual dimension. But my research into the brain and cognition goes a long way toward "explaining" art appreciation. I and my colleagues identify universal aesthetic principles, and then show how and why such principles evolved in the human brain. Does this have any bearing on the view that the creative spark is simply a manifestation of the divine spark in us all?

Indian artists often speak of conveying the rasa or "essence" of something in order to evoke a specific emotional response in the brain of the observer. What does that mean?

One clue comes from the "peak shift" effect. If a rat is taught to discriminate a square from a rectangle (of say, 3 to 2 aspect ratio) and is rewarded for the rectangle, it will soon learn to respond more frequently to the rectangle. Paradoxically, the rat's response to a rectangle that is even longer and skinnier (say, of aspect ratio 4 to 1) is even greater. This curious result implies that what the rat is learning is not a particular rectangle but a rule, namely, rectangularity.

How does this principle relate to human vision? Consider the way in which a skilled cartoonist produces a caricature of a famous face, say, Richard Nixon's. What the cartoonist does (unconsciously) is to take the average of all faces, subtract the average from Nixon's face (to get the difference between Nixon's face and all others), and then amplify the differences to produce a caricature. The final result, of course, is a drawing that is even more Nixon-like than the original.

The same principle applies to all aspects of form recognition. It might seem a bit strange to regard caricatures as art, but one has only to take a look at the accentuated hips and bust of the Chola bronze of Goddess Parvati, or the Venus "fertility" figures, to see at once that these are es-

124

sentially caricatures of the female form. There may be neurons in the brain that represent the sensuous, rotund feminine form as opposed to the angular masculine form. The artist has chosen to amplify the "very essence" of being feminine by moving the image even further toward the feminine end of the female/male spectrum.

Ethologists have long known that a seagull chick will beg for food by pecking at its mother's beak. Remarkably, it will peck just as vigorously at a yellow stick with a red dot at the end (the gull's beak has a vivid red spot near the tip). Indeed, a very long, thin yellow stick, with three red stripes at the end has been found to be even more effective in eliciting pecks. The gull's form-recognition areas are obviously wired in such a way that the long stick is producing a superstimulus, or a caricature in "beak space." If there were an art gallery in the world of the seagull, this "superbeak" would doubtless qualify as a great work of art—a Picasso.

Likewise, given how little we know about the encoding of form in the human brain, it is possible that contemporary art is the equivalent—for humans—of the stick with three red stripes, producing peak shifts in form-detecting areas in our brains. (And, analogously, a van Gogh or a Monet may represent a caricature in "color space" rather than "form space.")

A second important aesthetic principle is "grouping." Paintings often have identical colors scattered in different parts of the canvas. Every fashion designer knows that if you wear a red scarf, then you should have some red in your skirt to create a pleasing resonance. But why should this be aesthetically pleasing? Since vision evolved mainly to find objects, grouping may facilitate this. For example, if you see a partially obscured lion through green foliage, your visual areas link all the yellow splotches and bind them together to delineate the lion's outline. One's brain processes have seen to it that the very process of binding and dis-covery is pleasing. So here, again, we have an artist's rule of thumb that can be explained in terms of both evolution and brain anatomy.

Last, why is an outline drawing so much more evocative than a full-color photo? One suggestion is that this is because the visual centers in the brain have limited attentional resources. What is critical to recogniz-ing Nixon's face is its outline. Its color, skin texture, hair, and so forth, are, after all, like those of any other person. So the extra information in a photo actually distracts your attentional resources from where the real action is. We call this the principle of isolation.

These ideas can be tested experimentally. Ordinarily when we look at something evocative, our palms start sweating and this can be measured as a change in skin conductance. You would show a big response to a lion or a pinup, but not to a chair. But if our theory is right, then you would get an even bigger response to a drawing of a lion (or better still a cari-cature) than to a color photo! Either way, one has a direct, objective mea-sure of one's emotional response to art.

Some find such scientific investigations of the "laws" of artistic expe-rience disturbing. I do not see why. Though such laws might have origi-nated out of our evolutionary past, art retains its spiritual dimension. The development of a "science" of art takes nothing away from its also occupying a celestial realm.

The psychoanalyst Ethel Person has said: "Half beast, half angel, Man has been described as a paradoxical creature. We are each condemned not only to death and extinction but—and this is what renders our con-dition tragic—to knowledge of our mortality. It is the dichotomy be-tween the dross of our bodies and the immortal stuff of our souls that makes us crave transcendence."

The ultimate goal of art—whether Eastern or Western—is to help us achieve such transcendence.

●

Vilayanur Ramachandran is director of the Center for Research on Brain and Cognition at the University of California, San Diego; he is editor in chief of the four-volume Encyclopedia of Human Behavior.

Part Eight

Personhood and the Soul

Modern science describes us in terms of genes, or chemical and electrical flows in the brain, or as evolved animals. Artificial intelligence (AI) research aims to construct machines that are like us. Throughout, the emphasis is on the physical. So what has become of the soul—that which confers upon us "personhood" and engages in a relationship with God? Is it any longer tenable to believe in a life that goes beyond our physical existence?

Malcolm Jeeves does not see himself as having a soul; rather, he is a soul. He tackles the question of the possible "soulishness" of the other animals.

John Polkinghorne draws on complexity theory; we are more than the sum of our individual parts. The totality of what we are has a pattern to it; in computerspeak, it has *information*. Though that information is currently embodied in physical form, it does not need that particular manifestation. Beyond our death, God can recall the pattern that was us and re-create it in some other life.

Do robots have souls? Though present-day models are probably too primitive to be thought of in that way, **Anne Foerst** sees no reason why future robots, of the appropriate degree of complexity, should be excluded. Indeed, she regards her work in AI as a positive help to her in thinking through what it means for us humans to be made in the image of God.

Closely related to the idea of having, or being, a soul is that of becoming self-consciously responsible moral persons. **Henry Thompson** reflects on how we achieve such a status. If it is through adults imbuing children with a moral sensibility (or awakening a God-given disposition thereto), perhaps we ought to be doing the same for robots. What form should "computational morality" take?

129

Whatever Became of the Soul?

MALCOLM JEEVES

"You, your joys, and sorrows are no more than the behaviour of a vast assembly of nerve cells and their associated molecules," wrote Nobel laureate Francis Crick. "The idea that man has a disembodied soul is as unnecessary as the old idea that there was a life force," and this, Crick believes, "is in head-on contradiction to the religious beliefs of billions of human beings alive today." More recently, *Nature Neuroscience* editorialized: "The rapid progress of neuroscience has . . . deep and possibly disturbing implications"; its findings are "interpreted by some as providing new ammunition for a materialist account of human nature, and thus as an attack on traditional belief systems."

Few neuroscientists any longer believe that humans are composed of two distinct and separable parts, called brain and mind, or body and soul. With every neuroscience advance comes further confirmation of the inseparable bond between brain and mind. In *Descartes's Error*, the neuroscientist Antonio Damasio contends that the distinction between the diseases of "brain" and "mind" is an unfortunate cultural inheritance that reflects ignorance of the actual brain/mind relationship.

But what about the soul? It's true that many people of faith continue to speak and sing words that assume that our human nature includes an entity called a soul that interacts with our bodies but leaves at our death. This body/soul dualism—the legacy of Plato, St. Augustine, and René Descartes—cannot be ruled out on scientific grounds. Another Nobel laureate, Sir John Eccles, believed that mind and soul are indeed non-material entities that interact with the physical body. Many adherents of New Age religion and devotees of parapsychology hold a similar view.

As a neuroscientist and Christian, I do not, however, feel led by either my science or my faith to believe that I am made up of two separate entities, body and soul. Rather, I believe I am a unified living being (which is one translation of *soul* found in some modern versions of the Bible), with physical and mental aspects. The mental dimension of my being is as important as the physical body/brain on which it depends. Indeed, the emerging scientific evidence, fueled by psychology's so-called cognitive revolution, gives as much weight to the mental aspect of our nature as to the physical.

As the past century of Jewish and Christian biblical scholarship reminds us, our "soulishness" can be understood as our relatedness to God, to other humans, and to all of creation. The biblical idea is remarkably similar to the neuroscience view that we are psychosomatic unities, not dualistic packages. I do not *have* a soul, I *am* a living being or soul. People of faith should therefore pause before they rush to the barricades to defend their beliefs in the soul against what they see as the latest scientific effort to reduce everything to physical explanation.

But what about the animals? If humans do not possess a separate "thing" called the soul or mind, is there no difference between humans and other animals? We share more than 98 percent of our DNA with the apes. As many programs on "animal minds" have reminded us, animals can think and solve problems. Do they also possess "soulishness"?

Support for such an idea comes from an unlikely source. The opening chapters of the Hebrew and Christian Scriptures refer to both animals and humans. However, the evidence accumulated by psychologists makes it clear that animals differ greatly from humans in "soulishness"—so much so that the difference seems qualitative. This is surely evidenced in the absence of libraries, observatories, nuclear science laboratories, and high-tech medical procedures among chimps.

An analogy may help. The same materials, when mixed in different proportions, can behave quite differently. A weak mixture of gas and air may contain the same molecules as a richer mixture that burns. Below a certain minimum concentration, the mixture is simply nonflammable. Similarly, a complex human brain embodies conscious mental and spiritual qualities not found in animals. Humans, it seems, have the critical capacities for personal relatedness, for complex language, for forming a "theory of mind," for historical memory, and for contemplating the future. Such highly developed "soulishness" makes humans unique and, I believe, confers the capacity for personal relationship with God.

To defend human dignity, we do not need to assume Plato's pre-Christian idea of an immortal soul or to denigrate animals. Both humans and other animals are part of the creation of the one who knows even when a sparrow falls.

•

Malcolm Jeeves, C.B.E., is Research Professor of Psychology at the University of St. Andrews and President of the Royal Society of Scotland. He is the author of Whatever Became of the Soul? *and, with Sam Berry,* Science, Life and Christian Belief.

More Than a Body?

JOHN POLKINGHORNE

What am I? A smart tap on the head with a hammer will show that I'm dependent on my body. But am I just a body? Is there a spiritual bit of me, too? Have I got a soul?

For much of the past two thousand years, people thought of themselves as apprentice angels. The "real me" was a spiritual component, trapped in a body but awaiting release at death. At the start of the third millennium, that's an increasingly difficult belief to hold. Studies of brain damage and the effects of drugs show how dependent our personalities are on the state of our bodies. Charles Darwin has taught us that our ancestry is the same as that of other animals. Earth was once lifeless, and life seems to have emerged from complex chemical interactions. Many scientists think that we are nothing but collections of molecules.

Yet that's a pretty odd belief, too. Could mere chemicals write Shakespeare's plays or compose Handel's *Messiah* (or discover the laws of chemistry, for that matter)? There's something more to us than the merely material. But whatever that extra is, it is intimately connected with our bodies. We are a kind of package deal, mind and body closely related and not wholly detachable from each other. It's a puzzle to understand this. Oddly enough, the clue we need may be found in watching water being heated in a saucepan.

If the heat is applied gently, the water circulates from the bottom in a remarkable pattern. Instead of just flowing about any old how, it forms a pattern of six-sided cells, rather like in a beehive. This is an astonishing phenomenon. Trillions of molecules have to collaborate and move together in order to generate the pattern. The effect is a simple example of a new aspect of nature that scientists are just beginning to learn about. They call it complexity theory.

Physicists naturally started by studying the simplest systems available. They are the easiest to understand. Recently, the use of high-speed computers has extended our scientific range, and it is now possible to think about quite complicated situations. As this began to be explored, an unexpected realization dawned. Very often these complex systems turn out to have a quite simple overall behavior, ordered in some striking pattern—just like those trillions of molecules moving together in the saucepan.

The way physicists traditionally thought was in terms of the bits and pieces that make up a complex system. The exchanges of energy between these bits and pieces look extremely complicated. However, it turns out that if you think about the system as a whole, there can be these remarkably orderly patterns of behavior. In other words, there are two levels of description. One involves energy and bits and pieces. The other involves the whole system and pattern. At this second level, using computer-speak, we can say that what we need to think about is the *information* that specifies the pattern.

What has this got to do with the human soul? Whatever the soul may be, it is surely the "real me," linking that little boy of sixty years ago with the aging academic of today. That real me is certainly not the matter of my body. That is changing all the time, through eating and drinking, wear and tear. We have very few atoms in our bodies that were there five years ago. What provides the continuity is the almost infinitely complex pattern in which that matter is organized. That pattern is the soul, the real me.

So what do religious people make of that? Actually, they got there first! The Hebrews of Old Testament times never thought of human

135

beings as apprentice angels. Instead, they took the package deal view that we are bodies full of life. The greatest thinker of medieval Christianity, St. Thomas Aquinas, thought the same. He was greatly influenced by the ideas of Aristotle. For Aristotle, the soul was the "form" (that is, pattern) of the body.

But, if the soul isn't a detachable spiritual part of us, what hope do we have of a destiny beyond death? Won't that wonderful pattern that is you or that is me be dissolved at our deaths—and that's that? If this is how you think, you have forgotten to take God into account. Our real hope that death is not the end depends on our belief in the trustworthiness of God. If we matter to God now—and we certainly do—we shall matter to God forever. We shall not be cast aside like broken pots on some cosmic rubbish heap. Human beings are not naturally immortal, but the faithful God will give us a destiny beyond our deaths. It makes perfect sense to believe that God will remember the pattern that is you, or the pattern that is me, and re-create those patterns in the world to come. Christians call it resurrection. The true Christian hope has not been survival, but death followed by resurrection. Such a hope is as credible in the third millennium as it has been in the preceding two thousand years.

•

John Polkinghorne was formerly Professor of Mathematical Physics at Cambridge University and president of Queens College, Cambridge. He is the only ordained Fellow of the Royal Society and was knighted in 1997. Among his books are The Way the World Is, Reason and Reality, *and* Science and Creation.

Robot: Child of God

ANNE FOERST

Do robots have souls? Probably not—at least not the ones that have so far been built. But what of the future?

The aim of those of us who do research in artificial intelligence (AI) is to construct a machine with humanlike intelligence. We dream of Commander Data, the fictional hero of the Starship *Enterprise*. What a piece of engineering! How wonderful to build a robot like that. Should that prove feasible, I for one would regard him (or it) as having the attributes of personhood and dignity just like ourselves. He would be a child of God.

In one of the episodes of *Star Trek*, the *Enterprise* crew decides that Data is so useful to them that it is desirable to have more of the same. They decide to disassemble him to find out how he works, then rebuild him and produce copies. Data is at first intrigued by the idea, but then realizes that the procedure is less than safe. Fearing for his own existence, he decides to resign from the *Enterprise* command. Here the question of Data's personhood comes up: *Can* he even resign? Does he have the right to choose, or is he merely a machine without any rights—the property of Star Fleet?

The arguments go back and forth. The discussion boils down to the question of whether or not Data has a soul. Indeed, do we ourselves have "souls"? The final decision is that Data has as much right as we do to search for his own soul. Data participates in the human community; he has friends and a sexual relationship; he is loved as a person and is not regarded by most crew members as a mere machine. Any robot which is like us, and is accepted by humans as one of us, is a person.

Much has been written about the anthropomorphization of tools such as cars and stereos. Today, electronic gadgets like Tamagotchies or Furbies continue this trend. People in Western societies are quite willing to treat as living beings certain machines displaying social behaviors like

Tamagotchie's hunger or Furbie's "learning" of language. Because of this trend, AI researchers, most of them fans of *Star Trek* anyway, usually agree with the judgment that Data is a person. They base this on the way people accept technologies into their lives and are willing to create a society in which technology and humans play interdependent and mutually benefiting roles.

At the same time, the researchers see themselves as a safeguard against too much projection. Since they understand and repair the machines and know exactly how they function, they are much less likely to treat them as *more* than they actually are. They warn against too much anthropomorphization and define the borders between gadgets and persons. They are those most likely to know when a machine oversteps the boundary and becomes something "more than a machine."

But what could this mythical "more than" be? In the Jewish and Christian tradition, human specialness is symbolized in the metaphor that humans are created in the image of God (Genesis 1:26, 27). The majority of Jewish and Christian theologians have attempted to identify the divine part of humankind with particular empirical features: our creativity; our use of language, logic, and reason; the human ability to think in an abstract way; even our humor, or just the way we look.

But I see it differently. Theology today often concentrates on the biblical testimony that the concept of God should incorporate aspects of both man and woman. This metaphor illustrates that we are images of God only within gender relationships, or to put it more generally, within functioning and beneficial communications. This process of continuing communication, of relationship and interaction, is what makes us images of God. God's promise to start and maintain a relationship with us by creating us in God's image enables us to create community and to live wholesome relationships.

In this metaphorical and communicative interpretation of the creation of humans, God's promise marks the beginning of the relationship between God and humans and between man and woman. It is God's promise, and not some empirical feature, which makes us special and gives us a specific role within creation. It is God's creation of us that assigns value and personhood to each individual.

In the light of this understanding of human specialness, I would have a hard time not to assign personhood to a creature possessing the appropriate degree of complexity. If a being is understood as a partner and friend, it seems hard to take this attribute of value, assigned to it by its friends, away. Instead of insisting on a qualitative difference between us and the machines AI will create, it seems more reasonable to turn the question around. Not reflections on "why a machine never can become like us," but instead the question of what might be the conditions under which God would accept such a creature as God's child. Then we will recognize the arrogance some people display when denying dignity to other creatures.

God's promise to creation is universal—this is the biblical tradition. It is not our place to exclude people from the community, be it because of their race, their gender, their capabilities, or their worldviews. The reflections about Commander Data as a child of God might help us to remember in humility that each and every person's value is grounded not in his or her abilities but in God's promise and in that alone. The fictional Data might thus serve as a thinking tool to prepare us for the AI machines to come.

Anne Foerst is a postdoctoral fellow in the Artificial Intelligence Laboratory at the Massachusetts Institute of Tecnology, a research associate at Harvard Divinity School, and director of the MIT/Boston Theological Institute's God and Computers project.

Computers and Morality

HENRY THOMPSON

How about installing a new kind of magistrate on the bench—a robot? Such a judge would be unbiased by reason of social affinity or antipathy, undistracted by tiredness or migraine. Possessed of a letter-perfect memory for all statutes and precedents, it would apply this knowledge precisely. In short, it would be the ideal magistrate: knowledgeable and dispassionate.

Or is there something missing? Even supposing we could overcome the very real difficulties standing in the way of creating a computer with all those properties, surely a crucial component of our willingness to submit to judgment is the unspoken, perhaps even unthought, assumption that the judge is morally responsible. Could such a robot be regarded as responsible? Indeed, what does it mean to think of ourselves as being responsible?

Machines acting as independent agents may sound like science fiction, but their forerunners are now among us. Computer systems already in place have a degree of autonomy and potential impact on us that should serve as a wake-up call that deep and serious moral questions are involved.

There are many concerned scientists who have warned of substantial moral choices involved in empowering computer systems with the potential for significant harm (or benefit) to human beings. Computers are already in more or less unsupervised control of landing airplanes in the fog, calculating and administering radiation therapy, and stocking warehouses. We even came quite close, in the early 1980s, to putting a fully automatic launch control system in place for the nuclear missiles based in Western Europe.

There are some statutory controls in place, for instance, in the aircraft industry. But the issues involved need to be understood by the general public and responded to more systematically by government.

But a more intriguing and uplifting prospect emerges from the confrontation of machines and morality: perhaps we can learn something about the origins and nature of *our own* moral sensibilities by a consideration of computational morality.

Returning to our hypothetical robot magistrate, we required it to be responsible. This means more than being responsible for its administration of justice in the same sense that El Niño is responsible for storms; we also require it to be *self-consciously* responsible—it should be accountable; it should take responsibility.

Taking responsibility is an aspect of personal morality. What we're really demanding here is that the mechanical magistrate be a recognizably moral agent. So what would it take for a computer to become a real moral agent?

Well, how does *anyone* become a real moral agent? Is *become* even the right word here? Some would certainly argue that moral agency is intimately connected with the essence of being human—with the soul—and that it's a manifestation of divine grace. From this perspective there could never be a nonhuman moral agent (unless by a similar act of grace!). If we think that moral agency is something which *can* be acquired—indeed, that one of the major responsibilities of parents is to help their children acquire it—then we may legitimately ask if our mechanical magistrate might acquire it, too.

Not surprisingly, this leads to the question of how children acquire the status of moral agents, supposing that they in fact do. The most obvious answer is that they obtain it by participating in a community of moral agents who provide both an implicit model and explicit instruction. And this seems to me to turn into an insurmountable problem for computers. We allow children to participate in families and society at large as part of their acculturation process. This is a means of imbuing them with a moral sensibility (or alternatively of stimulating/awakening a God-given disposition thereto). We allow them to do this because we have the most personal possible evidence that they are capable of moral agency—we were once like them ourselves, and we managed it.

What evidence would it take to convince us that constructed artifacts, as opposed to flesh of our flesh, should be allowed that opportunity? This is a chicken-and-egg problem for which there is no obvious way out: it's not dispassionate computers we want, but compassionate ones—ones we've grown up with, and which therefore share our values.

The kinds of questions raised here illustrate what the study of computational morality might mean. We're using the thought experiment of the creation of a mechanical magistrate to probe our own self-understanding with respect to fundamental moral questions.

There are other aspects of our moral and spiritual life in which such an approach might bear fruit: the nature of decisions and the question of free will (what actually happens when a computer "decides" to sell stock or prescribe a course of treatment), even euthanasia (the famous question of turning off a supposedly sentient computer).

Another encouraging thing about this idea of computational morality is that it's not just for the theologians and the academics. The kind of armchair exploration that arises from consideration of examples such as the mechanical magistrate is engaging for anyone (indeed, Isaac Asimov wrote a whole series of stories nearly fifty years ago employing precisely this approach).

Increasingly, science seems to be taken to be synonymous with secular humanism. So it's encouraging for scientists who do have a strong religious commitment to see a way to use our science to make investigation of our moral and spiritual natures a vivid and enlightening activity available to anyone.

•

Henry Thompson is Reader in the Department of Artificial Intelligence and the Centre for Cognitive Science at the University of Edinburgh. His area of research is language and speech processing, and he is involved in promoting awareness of the moral and social implications of AI research.

Part Nine

 Quantum Physics and Relativity

Our everyday experience leads us to conclude that there is a strict causal connection between events. Quantum physics shows this not to be the case—at least in regard to subatomic events. From any given state of affairs one can predict only the probabilities of a variety of possible outcomes; at this level, chance rules. **David Bartholomew** reflects on what this, and other examples of the role of chance in nature, might imply for the idea of a purposive God.

Quantum physics throws up various paradoxes. These challenge us to inquire more deeply into the types of questions we can ask of the physical world and the kinds of answers it is reasonable to expect. Are we up against the barrier of the knowable here, as some physicists contend? **Russell Stannard** draws a parallel between the discussions led by Niels Bohr and Albert Einstein into the interpretation of quantum physics, and earlier debates over the Trinitarian nature of the Christian God and the paradox of Jesus being both God and man.

In response to the controversies over quantum theory, Einstein once declared that "God does not play dice." **Nancy Abrams** and **Joel Primack** examine the modern physicists' use of the term *God*.

Besides quantum theory, the other great development in physics in the first part of the twentieth century was the theory of relativity. At high speed, observers in relative motion do not agree on the values of spatial distances or of time intervals. These differing conclusions reveal a hitherto unsuspected link between space and time—a link so close we now regard time as the fourth dimension. The explanation of these differing perceptions is that spatial distances and time intervals are but three-dimensional and one-dimensional projections, respectively, of a reality that is in truth four-dimensional; they are but appearances. **Sir John Houghton** uses this analogy of higher dimensionality as a tool for opening up our thinking about the nature of God.

God or Chance?

DAVID BARTHOLOMEW

Chance appears to have replaced God as the explanation for much that happens. The world in which God was presumed to control every detail has gone forever.

Wherever we look the story seems to be the same. In physics, for example, the solidity of stones and tables dissolves into the bizarre world of quantum theory—when viewed on a small enough scale. This is a world in which there is an inescapable uncertainty in how things develop.

In biology, the course of evolution depends crucially on accidents of reproduction. Indeed, it is over the role of chance in evolution that belief in a controlling God has taken the hardest knocks. Writers like Richard Dawkins see God as unnecessary; chance and accident do it all.

If these writers are correct, there appears very little left for any God to do. So, is there any longer a point in trying to retain a place for a God who is supposed to be in charge? After all, in previous battles, science always seems to have won. Would it not be better to recognize the inevitable and retire gracefully?

Retreat would be premature, first, because it is mistaken to suppose that chance is inconsistent with order and purpose. On the contrary, some of life's greatest certainties are built on chance.

For instance, boy and girl babies are born in roughly equal numbers. But this is not because sex has to be determined on an individual basis by heavenly edict. Instead, it results from something more like the toss of a coin. This is a simple way of ensuring that roughly equal numbers of the two sexes are born—in the long run.

The same principle underpins the insurance industry. Whether our particular home is destroyed by fire next year is unpredictable. But the number of such fires nationally is near enough certain for insurance companies to make a good living. In the same manner, mathematicians solve some of their most intractable problems by using sophisticated versions of the coin-tossing idea. The production of what are called random numbers for this purpose is big mathematical business.

Thus, uncertainty at one level can lead to certainty at another.

Of course, not all chance happenings in nature get averaged out in this fashion. Sometimes a one-off random occurrence can have crucial long-term consequences. A single event way back in the evolutionary family tree, for example, might have played a determining role in whether or not humans would eventually appear on Earth. Again, the chance impact of a meteorite can wipe out whole species—as is believed to have happened to the dinosaurs.

But even in such cases, one can still point to a way in which certainty may emerge from uncertainty. There may be many paths to essentially the same end; if one avenue is closed, others remain. There are certainly examples of similar creatures with different ancestral histories—as with placental and marsupial mammals. Further, the randomness itself may serve an evolutionarily useful purpose. By creating variety it may make it more likely that there will be some survivors of any catastrophe capable of living in the new environment. Indeed, there is good and growing evidence from current research that the complexity needed to support life may be an inevitable consequence of primeval chaos. Chance may well be a necessary ingredient of the recipe for producing life.

From this viewpoint, chance is not an alternative to God but something one might expect him to know about and use. After all, if it is such an elegant way of producing a living world, we should not be surprised if it was part of his tool kit. God does not have to fashion "each tiny flower that opens" in minutest detail. He goes one better and creates a system with the potential for self-creation.

One thing about which we are certain is that intelligent life has appeared in at least one place in the universe. It follows that, in the beginning, the chance of life occurring somewhere could not have been zero —otherwise we should not be here. If there were many sites where it could happen, then, in such a vast universe, it is likely that life would arise sometime, somewhere.

But does all of this make it any easier to see how God might actually do things, like answer prayer?

In their eagerness to retain a role for God, some believers have supposed that if we can see no reason for something happening, then God must be directly responsible. The chance at the heart of the atom is then seen as one place where God may be pulling the strings.

The modern mathematical theory of chaos lends some credence to this idea because it shows that undetectable perturbations to a system can have major consequences. Without us knowing, it could therefore be quite easy for God, who understands how it all works, to manipulate things on the small scale to produce effects which we can observe.

Perhaps. But it is not clear whether this method of control would actually work in a system as complicated as our universe.

Maybe God's way of acting is as mysterious as our own. After all, we really have little idea of how our own intentions arise and are translated into actions. When we have solved that problem, we might be better placed to tackle the bigger question of how God does it.

•

David Bartholomew is Emeritus Professor of Statistics at the London School of Economics, of which he was also pro-director. He is, in addition, a Fellow of the British Academy, a former president of the Royal Statistical Society, and an ordained Methodist preacher. Bartholomew is the author of God of Chance *and* Uncertain Belief.

Paradoxes in Science and Theology

RUSSELL STANNARD

What is light? What is matter? Perfectly reasonable questions to ask—so one might think. But all is not what it seems. Many scientists believe that such questions are not only difficult to answer, they have no answers *at all*. If they are right, then fundamental physics begins to look a little like theology.

Our story begins in the early part of the twentieth century. Light was discovered to have a dual nature. Some experiments pointed to its being a wave; others to its being a stream of particles. But that is odd: how can something be both a spread-out wave—like a succession of ripples on a pond—and at the same time a small localized particle—like a tiny billiard ball?

A similar apparent contradiction arose when a study was made of the ultimate constituents of matter. They too exhibited both wave and particle aspects.

No way out of this dilemma could be found until Niels Bohr, the Danish physicist, came up with a remarkable suggestion. He claimed that science tells us nothing at all about the world as it is in itself; it does not answer questions of the form "What is . . . ?" Instead, it tells us of the way we *interact* with the world.

Thus concepts like "wave" and "particle" apply not to objects themselves (light or matter) but to how we interact with them. There are wave-like interactions and particle-like interactions, and that is all we can say. It being physically impossible to perform both types of experiment at the same time, there is never a need to invoke both concepts simultaneously. Provided we stick solely to our interactions or observations of nature, there is no paradox.

Bohr went on to assert that this ability to speak meaningfully only of our interactions was no temporary restriction. This was the frontier of the knowable—a barrier that would never be breached.

This claim was made in the late 1920s, and it did not go unchallenged. Leading the counterattack was Albert Einstein. As the arguments flowed back and forth, more and more physicists came to side with Bohr, despite the fact that no one relished the idea of being in the opposite camp to Einstein! In the years that have ensued since those heated debates, no one has yet come up with a convincing description of the world as it is in itself, divorced from our observation of it—which is what Bohr would have expected.

But enough of the modern paradoxes of physics. What has this to do with theology?

Paradox has been a feature of Christian theology from earliest times. In trying to answer the question Who, or what, is God? the church fathers came to the conclusion that they had to regard him as Father, Son, and Holy Spirit. Nevertheless, he was one God, not three. Moreover, each of the Persons of this Trinity was not to be thought of as merely a part, or aspect, of God; each was fully God. Difficult though it was to see how the apparent contradiction was to be reconciled, they considered any simpler description of God would not do justice to the totality of the evidence.

When later they came to consider Who is Jesus? they concluded he was both fully God and fully man—omnipotent, omnipresent God, and at the same time limited, localized man—another paradox. Thus in Christian theology one deals with paradoxes every bit as puzzling as those that have now surfaced in physics.

It was in response to these paradoxes that Gregory Palamas, the fourteenth-century Archbishop of Thessalonica, decided that God was absolutely unknowable in his "essence," that is to say, as he was in himself. Instead, he was to be knowable only through his "energies"—the ways he revealed himself through the three Persons—the ways he interacted with us.

Much the same theme was taken up by, among others, the Danish theologian Søren Kierkegaard. Pondering the same Christian doctrines, he concluded that there were two kinds of truth: objective and subjective truth. When the truth appeared from an objective point of view to be paradoxical, it was an indication, he said, that one should be seeking a more subjective kind of truth—one involving one's own participation.

According to this particular strand of theological thought, one finds it necessary, as in modern physics, to take a step back from the objects of one's inquiry—whether they be God and Jesus, or light and matter—and be content to speak only of one's interactions with those objects.

As a postscript, I ought to point out that Bohr was an avid reader of his compatriot Kierkegaard. Could it be that twentieth-century physics owes a modest debt to a nineteenth- century theologian's contemplation of a fourth-century Christian creed?

•

Russell Stannard, O.B.E., is Emeritus Professor of Physics at the Open University, UK, and former vice president of the Institute of Physics in London. He is also a reader in the Anglican Church and author of Science and Wonders, The God Experiment, *and the best-selling* Uncle Albert *books.*

Einstein's View of God

NANCY ABRAMS AND
JOEL PRIMACK

Did Albert Einstein believe in God?

In 1992, when astronomer George Smoot announced the discovery of ripples in the heat radiation still arriving from the Big Bang, he said it was "like seeing the face of God." A somewhat more modest astrophysicist, whose theory had correctly predicted the discovery, was quoted as calling the ripples "the handwriting of God." Are these references to the Creator sacrilegious or legitimate interpretations? Either way, they are part of a search that Einstein began—the search for language to communicate the sacred dimension of doing science.

When Neils Bohr and others were developing quantum theory, it was spiritually unacceptable to Einstein that the ultimate nature of reality was randomness. "The [quantum] theory yields much," he wrote to quantum physicist Max Born in 1926, "but it hardly brings us close to the secrets of the Ancient One. In any case, I am convinced that He does not play dice." Generations of physicists have been profoundly influenced by the faith of the man who wrote, "I am a deeply religious nonbeliever. . . . This is a somewhat new kind of religion."

Recently an article in the magazine *Nature* reported the results of a survey that was first taken eighty years ago and repeated in 1996. In 1916, 40 percent of American scientists had said they believed in God. People who assume God is incompatible with science were surprised that the percentage of scientists who answered yes in 1996 was the same. They expected far fewer.

But if the question had been worded differently, there might have been even more. Einstein and the many scientists who are his spiritual companions were excluded, since the poll asked scientists if they believed in a personal God who answered prayers.

To Einstein the concept of a personal God was the main source of conflict between science and religion. God was not a father, king, or confidant. Nor was God the source of morality to Einstein. "The foundation of morality should not be made dependent on myth nor tied to any authority," he warned, "lest doubt about the myth or about the legitimacy of the authority imperil the foundation of sound judgment and action." Ethical behavior, he wrote, "should be based on sympathy, education, and social ties and needs; no religious basis is necessary."

What kind of God, then, did Einstein believe in? "I believe in Spinoza's God who reveals himself in the harmony of all that exists, but not in a God who concerns himself with the fate and actions of human beings."

The rock of Einstein's faith was that the world is rational. The fact is, the world doesn't have to be rational. It can't be proved to be. But to Einstein, what made science possible was this faith: causes lead to effects, not by anyone's changeable will, but by the operation of natural laws.

For him the greatest sacrilege was belief in miracles. If miracles were possible, then knowledge of truth was impossible because there would be no truth. He felt no awe for a willful, humanlike God but for the brilliant simplicity of the laws that have guided the evolution of the universe. "Whoever has undergone the intense experience of successful advances made in [science]," he wrote, "is moved by profound reverence for the rationality made manifest in existence."

He named this special reverence "cosmic religious feeling . . . which knows no dogma and no God conceived in man's image." Cosmic religious feeling he defined as awareness of a "spirit manifest in the laws of the Universe—a spirit vastly superior to that of man." This awareness, he believed, was "the strongest and noblest motivation for scientific research." And scientific research to him was "the only creative religious activity of our time." Which may be Einstein's theory of why great scientists so often feel drawn to the imagery of God: those who experience cosmic religious feeling will tend to be more deeply dedicated to their work and thus more likely to become great scientists.

Was Einstein's spiritual objection to quantum theory correct? Smoot's discovery and the subsequent observations of ripples in the cosmic background radiation say no. The creation of the largest structures in the universe the galaxies and the great clusters and superclusters of galaxies—was a random quantum process. If these results are confirmed by observations now in progress, then Einstein was wrong. Dice is God's favorite game. In his prejudice against this physical possibility, perhaps Einstein did not quite live up to his own faith: "no dogma." It now seems that God plays dice, but the universe is nevertheless rational because the game has rules.

The sacred dimension of science is a subject most scientists today avoid. They may fear misunderstanding and judgment by colleagues. Perhaps they have never really thought through their own ideas. Einstein's outspokenness on his religious attitude was rare. Today science is attacked both by postmodern philosophers claiming that all truths are relative (a horrendous misuse of Einstein's concept) and by creationists claiming that their metaphor is absolute truth. Under these circumstances, there are good reasons most scientists avoid all possibility of confusion with religion by never using terms suggestive of divinity.

But the price we pay is that there is no way to communicate an awesome reality: we are actually answering questions today whose very asking used to be a religious act. The astrophysicist who described the cosmic ripples as "the handwriting of God" is a coauthor of this essay. When we interpret the ripples in the cosmic background radiation, we are reading God's journal of the first days. What human action could be more sacred than that?

•

Nancy Abrams is a lawyer, writer, and composer/performer; she lectures on cosmology and culture at the University of California, Santa Cruz.

Joel Primack is Professor of Physics at the University of California, Santa Cruz; he is a cosmologist and co-inventor of the theory of cold dark matter.

Where Is God? Thinking in More Than Three Dimensions

 JOHN HOUGHTON

When the first Russian cosmonauts went up into space they reported back that they had not found God "up there." But did we expect them to? The taunt was naive. Nevertheless, it raised a serious challenge: where, in fact, is God?

To answer such a question demands that we use our imagination. Drawing on my background as a scientist, I find it helpful to imagine God as present in another dimension. Let me explain.

We are familiar with our 3-D world with three dimensions of space, North-South, East-West, and up-down. But we can think of time as having a dimension, too. Albert Einstein's new idea in his theory of relativity was to call time the fourth dimension to be added to the three dimensions of space. Coming right at the beginning of the twentieth century, this new view of time created a remarkable revolution in scientific thinking. Scientists now had a new picture of the universe—a 4-D world of space-time—that turned out to be a brilliant success. Today, scientists are constantly thinking in many dimensions.

To help us think what is meant by an extra dimension, try to imagine living in a 2-D world. Everything is flat. There is North-South and East-West but no up-down. Edwin Abbott, a mathematician of one hundred years ago, in a book called *Flatland*, worked out what life would be like for the Flatlanders. Their eyes could only look along the flat plane of Flatland. He made up rules by which they might recognize each other. Their houses were like plans on sheets of paper with no height and with doors like straight lines. They had no conception that there could be anything above or below their flat world. Above and below just did not exist.

The punch line of the book comes near the end. Abbott imagines a being like a round ball from 3-D "Spaceland" encountering Flatland and going through it. As the ball-shaped being enters Flatland, it first just touches it, then the being appears as a small circle, then a larger circle, then a smaller circle again before disappearing out the other side of Flatland. Flatlanders seeing this could not understand it at all. Where had the new being come from, and where had it gone to? The Spaceland being on its passages through Flatland appears again and again but fails to get across any message about the extra dimension. Eventually, in desperation the Spaceland being picks up one of the Flatlanders and they fly together over the plane of Flatland. They can see inside the Flatland houses. They can even see inside the bodies of the Flatland beings. The Flatlander is returned to Flatland and, now convinced, tries to explain to fellow Flatlanders what it is like to operate in a 3-D world. But they fail to understand. After all, there is no existence outside Flatland. They treat him as someone who has gone mad.

But we are rather like those Flatlanders. We live in our 4-D world of space-time with things we can touch and hear and see and events that we can experience. We imagine that is all there is. But suppose there is God out there in another dimension. Suppose this God makes himself known by interacting with—appearing within—our 4-D world. If we could find a window into such an extra dimension, that would be something very big indeed. It could create a revolution for us just like Einstein's new time dimension did for science.

Christianity claims just that. The God out there has entered our world in the person of Jesus. His life was remarkable. So was his death. Even more remarkable is the story of his resurrection from death. The accounts in the Bible describe how, to the amazement of his disciples, he had a new body which could appear and disappear at will. The appearances were just like those of the 3-D Spaceland being in 2-D Flatland.

All this would appear just fanciful if it were not that ever since that time people have experienced the living person of Jesus. How does this happen? They speak about a close personal relationship. It is as if they are not just imagining some remote being but experiencing him for real. And because God with the extra dimension is not limited by the dimensions of space or time, God has much greater freedom of action than we can conceivably know. Just try to imagine the capability possessed by a being outside time!

Talking about this extra God dimension is like having an analogy or a scientific "model." There is nothing new about such ways of thinking. The Hebrews in the Old Testament thought of God both as out there and within his people. The prophet Isaiah describes God who "dwells in the high and holy place, with him also that is of a contrite and humble spirit." Jesus in his teaching constantly used pictures and analogies; we call them parables. Scientists especially like to think in terms of models. In a world buzzing with scientific and technical language and jargon, metaphor and model from the world of science can help us gain a measure of understanding of other parts of our experience.

This analogy of God in a fifth dimension, beyond the 4-D world in which we live, really stimulates and stretches our thinking about where God is and how he acts. Just as a 3-D world is solid compared with the flimsy 2-D world of Flatland, so experiences which involve God in the extra spiritual dimension can be much more solid and real than the material world we know so well. A strong message is that I can bring God into my life and start to experience the fifth dimension now.

•

Sir John Houghton, C.B.E., F.R.S., was former head of the Meteorological Office, London; he is chairman of the Royal Commission on Environmental Pollution.

Part Ten

Limitations to Science

One cannot help but be impressed by the pace of scientific advance and the way it is transforming our world through technology. Such successes have led certain scientists to adopt a triumphalist stance, claiming their science to be the only sure route to knowledge and understanding. According to this view—known as "scientism"—other modes of investigation (religion, for example) can be dismissed as unnecessary and irrelevant.

George Ellis disagrees; he points out that, valuable though science is, it has its limitations. It is unable to speak meaningfully on subjects such as aesthetics and ethics, or on metaphysical and religious issues.

Taking up the same theme, **William Stoeger** stresses that science is powerless to address the question of the source of the very laws of nature it seeks to investigate. Not only that, but even when working within its own narrow compass, science provides understanding that is at best provisional. It follows that the claim sometimes made that modern science leaves no room for God to operate cannot be substantiated.

Robert Herrmann draws on the insights of Michael Polanyi and Thomas Kuhn to show that science is not as objective an activity as was once thought; understanding is always colored by the mind-set brought to the problem by the investigator—a mind-set influenced by social pressures within the scientific community. Kurt Gödel has provided a rigorous proof that there can be no such thing as a complete and consistent mathematical theory. Mathematics being the language of the physical sciences, we conclude the same must be true of physical theory. Such developments have fostered a new sense of humilty in scientific circles. This in turn is already leading to a closer convergence of scientific and religious thinking.

Are There Limitations to Science?

GEORGE ELLIS

Some writers claim that there are no limits to what science can do. They are either ignorant or are having you on.

Great progress has been made by science in the past century, and this underlies the technology that has transformed our lives. Flush toilets, washing machines, refrigerators, telephones, television, computers, CD players, jumbo jets, and laser surgery have resulted from this progress. Science has also led to profound new understanding about the world in which we live and the way our bodies work. We know about the expanding universe, continental drift, the many cycles in the biosphere on which life depends, the chemical and physical functioning of our body. We even understand a great deal about how our mind works—the underlying transfers of ions, the electrical impulses, the connectivity of neurons, and so on. No one imagined a century ago that today we would understand the molecular basis of heredity and know the genetic code. Given the boundaries science has already overcome, one might easily get the impression that it will find no limits in the future.

This idea is wrong. As our understanding of the universe develops, so does our understanding of the limits on what science will ever be able to do. I leave aside here the question of whether science is reaching its limits in many scientific areas (which may well be true). The point is that the scientific method itself has fundamental limits, and many important areas lie outside those limits.

One example is aesthetics. Suppose I were to produce a device looking like a video recorder, which I called an Aesthetic Meter. Imagine I make the following claim: if I point the meter at a picture, it produces a score on a screen—98 for a Rembrandt, 85 for a van Gogh, 20 for a Jackson Pollock, and so on, telling you precisely how beautiful the picture is. Would you believe it? Of course not! Beauty is not a quantity science can deal with; no known experiment is able to measure the beauty of a painting. That is not a scientific concept. The same holds for music, sculpture, poetry, literature, theater, dance: the whole world of aesthetics is beyond the scope of science. But it is of great importance to human life.

The same is true of ethics. Neither "good" nor "bad" is a scientifically measurable quality. We do not have a scientifically based scale, like the Richter scale for earthquakes, for morality: stealing a bicycle is −2 moral units, giving two hundred dollars to the poor is +5, and so on. Any claim to measure good or bad by some scientific experiment is rubbish. Science cannot tell you what is morally valuable. It cannot say if saving gray squirrels or minke whales is an ethical act—for this also is not a scientific category. What science can do is tell you what environmental policies are likely to save them from extinction. But there is no way it can tell you whether it is either just or good to let arctic fisherman make their living off seals and whales. That has to be determined on the basis of policy analysis informed by an ethical stance that comes from somewhere else—your religious beliefs, for instance. And the same limitation of science applies to many issues important to us. In the film *Contact*, at one point Elle is asked, "Did your father love you?" The response to her definite "Yes" is, "Prove it." She is silenced by this—for as a scientist, she knows that this is not something that science can prove, even though she knows it to be true.

Another category science cannot deal with is metaphysical issues. Underlying science is a series of such issues which cannot be probed by any scientific experiment. We know gravity exists, we can describe its effects, but we cannot tell you why it works. How indeed does the Earth pull the Moon, at that great distance? By a gravitational force? That is just a restating of the effect in new words, not an explanation in any fundamental sense. What is the reason that gravity holds matter under its spell and what enforces the rule that gravity is always attractive (unlike electromagnetism)? We do not know—if we did, we would be close to inventing an antigravity machine. What we can do is observe it in action and describe that action ever more accurately. We do not know how God or nature makes matter obey those rules. Science can tell you what the laws of physics are, but it cannot tell you why they exist. Science cannot tell you why the universe exists. And above all it cannot tell you whether or not God exists.

These limitations cannot be changed by future advances in science; they are fundamental to its nature. So we can expect many major advances in science in the future—in terms of understanding the future of the universe, the course of evolutionary history, the way the brain functions, for example—but we cannot expect it to solve ethical or moral or metaphysical issues. Science forms a valuable part of human life, but it is not the basis for a whole human life. We shall always need to study and teach ethics, aesthetics, and philosophy, as well as science—and this should include comparative religion if you want a whole human being. Those who claim science will supplant any or all of them are indulging in a little fantasy. Be kind to them, but don't take them seriously.

•

George Ellis is Professor of Applied Mathematics at the University of Capetown; he is the author of 240 scientific papers and ten books, including The Large Scale Structure of Space-Time with Stephen Hawking. A Quaker, Ellis is active in various social programs.

Can God Really Act in Our World and in Our Lives?

WILLIAM STOEGER

What does God do? If the answer is nothing, why should we believe in God at all?

From what science tells us it seems that everything that happens can be explained by the processes, regularities, and interrelationships described by physics, chemistry, and biology. There are no gaps in these laws of nature where God can tinker. Nature looks after itself. If this is true, then God is without a job—assuming there is a God in the first place.

But is it true? Leaving aside for the moment our scientific observations, our deeper experiences appear to indicate that as human persons we can make a difference; we have the freedom to live our lives how we wish. We do not feel that the way the world is fashioned prevents us from deciding to act in a manner of our own choosing. We exercise choice in the way we interact with other things and other people. There is enough play in the workings of nature to allow us to understand it, harness it for our purposes, and choose from among different alternatives.

Now, if that is the case for us mere humans, is it so unreasonable to expect that God could do the same?

Second, we need to recognize the limitations of science. We find that there are powerful experiences in our lives—of love, of wholeness, of truth and beauty, of meaning and value, of ultimate importance—experiences that take us beyond where science stops. These personal and community experiences somehow lead us to a belief that there is a God involved in our world and in our lives.

That is all very well, but is there any reason to trust such inclinations? A more careful and critical look at the sciences helps us resolve this dilemma. We can believe in God and in God's action in the world and in our lives—in history—and at the same time maintain what the sciences reveal.

The important point to recognize is that the sciences put to one side many of the important aspects of reality in order to understand certain basic processes, relationships, and structures in nature. The resulting knowledge about these underlying features of the world is very powerful—but also incomplete and provisional. There is, and always will be, a lot that we do not know, even about those things upon which science focuses its attention—gravity, matter, life, the human brain. The world, to say nothing of ourselves, is much more intricate and mysterious than the methods of science can unravel.

Science leaves out of its consideration any discussion of the *origin* of those laws and regularities—why they exist at all, or what meaning or significance they might have.

And what of questions to do with personal significance and value, of "the spirit," and of what may lie beyond death? These are also outside the limits of physics, chemistry, biology, and even psychology.

In light of the limits of science and the full range of our rich human experience, we can easily conceive of God acting in our world, in the world wonderfully described by the sciences. God acts not in supposed gaps in the laws of nature, but rather in and through the laws themselves. They are expressions of God's creative activity in nature. In some way God fashioned them to be what they are—what science discovers them to be. Then God uses them—including laws of chance, such as those involved in evolution by natural selection—in fashioning all that he creates. Or rather, God sustains creation in its automatic operation, letting it explore all its possibilities and become fully what it can be.

Finally, the many things that the sciences leave out of consideration, or cannot adequately describe, indicate that the laws of nature described by physics, chemistry, biology, and so on, are only a small, though significant, part of all the laws—the regularities, relationships, and processes—that actually function in the world. There are laws that are important for existence, for order, for persons in their interactions with each other, with nature, and, most important, with the perceived ground of meaning and value. These laws are just as important as those discovered by the sciences, and yet they are beyond what the sciences themselves can illuminate.

In summary, God acts through all the laws, including those which are beyond the competency of the sciences to explore. God acts through the laws of nature which all things obey—gravity, electromagnetism, chemical bonding, natural selection—to create and sustain all things in existence. These are by and large well, though imperfectly, described by the sciences.

But God also acts in a special way toward persons—in a personal way—through other persons, through special events and experiences, through communal life and in revelation. These involve laws of an order and depth which are outside the present and perhaps even the future limits of the sciences. But if we as persons act toward creation and toward one another in a similar way, is it so surprising that God should be able to do that also?

•

William Stoeger, S.J., is an astrophysicist-cosmologist at the Vatican Observatory, Castel Gandolfo, Italy, and at Tuscon, Arizona, and Associate Professor of Astronomy at the University of Arizona. He is the editor of the Philosophy in Science *series.*

Science and Religion: Converging Paths to Truth

ROBERT HERRMANN

Until a few decades ago, there was a popular notion that science was the only trustworthy path to truth. Other sources of truth, especially religious beliefs, were said to be outmoded. Now the situation is very different. It is no longer science which many people look to for answers. Hungering for deeper meaning, many have turned to religious truths.

Part of the reason for this change can be traced to the modern understanding of science itself. At its beginnings, science was viewed as a handmaiden of religion. The pioneers of science adopted the attitude that God had given them a world to be understood and appreciated through science in much the same way that theologians understood and appreciated God through the study of the Scriptures. But gradually, scientists began to believe that their methodology, based upon reason and experimentally verifiable fact, was sufficient in itself. The very success of science led to the gradual separation of science and religion.

Then, at the beginning of the twentieth century, the pendulum began to swing back. Physicists discovered a basic limitation in the measurement of the particles making up atoms. The idea that electrons orbited the atomic nucleus like planets orbiting the Sun was understood to be only a crude model. The orbits were replaced by smeared-out "probability clouds" which specified only the probability of finding the electron in various locations. The upshot of this limitation of measurement was puzzling. Events studied with individual particles like electrons were unpredictable, yet the physical system, containing many such particles, behaved in a precise mathematical way. The reaction of some scientists was annoyance and disagreement. Albert Einstein's response was that "God does not play dice."

Then cosmology revealed that the universe was bigger by many orders of magnitude than we had ever dreamed and that it had come to be by way of a "Big Bang," a powerful explosion which seemed to confirm the basic notion found in the first verses of Genesis that the universe originated at some point in the past; it had not always existed.

On the biological side, the origin of life proved to be quite subtle. There seemed to be a delicate and intricate balance in the structure of the cosmos necessary for the emergence of life. The conditions were so restricted as to be given a name: *the anthropic principle*. If life came about by purely mechanistic means, then it was on the basis of a special set of circumstances.

There were also some remarkable findings on the human brain. The combination of all the neurons and the multitude of connections between neurons make for a level of complexity that rivals the number of stars in the universe. In effect, there is a universe of complexity in our heads! Such complexity appears everywhere. As we probe more deeply into the universe, the more the mysteries multiply. The pursuit of science is like peeling an onion. Each layer removed reveals another layer, and another, and on and on.

In addition to this deepening complexity in the workings of science, there has also come a new understanding of the nature of scientific truth. The idea that scientific truth is arrived at without feeling or bias, based solely upon experimental data, has been shown to be a myth. The philosopher of science Michael Polanyi has shown that no truth is arrived at without the scientist assuming (or having faith in) a particular worldview. Accordingly, even in science, there is no such thing as abstract knowledge; it is always knowledge held by someone as a commitment. So the faith component, so important in religion, has its counterpart in science.

Then, just as our ability to make measurements has built-in limits, so also there appear to be limits to the mathematical descriptions we provide in science. The famous theorem of the Czech mathematician Kurt Gödel, proved in 1931, stated that it is not possible to demonstrate that any mathematical system is both consistent and complete. There must exist true statements that cannot be proved within the system. The physicist Freeman Dyson of Princeton's Institute for Advanced Study argues similarly that the laws of physics, having as they do a mathematical formulation, must also be inexhaustible.

Finally, another critique of science was raised with the publication in 1970 of the historian Thomas Kuhn's book, The Structure of Scientific Revolutions. Kuhn described scientific progress as a series of alternating periods of normality, in which an accepted broad conceptual framework or "paradigm" was applied, and periods of revolution in which these paradigms were shattered and replaced by new ones. Social scientists picked up on this idea, and some even went so far as to suggest that scientific truth was purely the product of complex social interactions, dependent upon the prevailing "worldview" of the scientists involved. It was as though scientists just got together and agreed on a definition of truth, a sort of conspiracy.

With science on the defensive, people have begun to rethink the importance of religious faith as a valid source of truth and meaning. Indeed, some prominent scientists are even writing books about God and suggesting that many new discoveries in science take us well beyond scientific interpretation, reaching instead into the realm of religion.

Many people would conclude that God has placed remarkable signs in the heavens, on Earth, and in us. Science, for decades standing aloof, now appears to be pointing to religious faith as an equally valid source of truth.

•

Robert Herrmann was formerly Professor of Chemistry at Gordon College in Wenham, Massachusetts, and executive director of the American Scientific Affiliation. He has coauthored, with John Templeton, The God Who Would Be Known and Is God the Only Reality?

Part Eleven

Science/Religion Dialogue

It is a commonly held view that science and religion are enemies. **Kitty Ferguson** and **Martinez Hewlett** point out some of the widespread misconceptions that lead to this assessment; they offer advice to young people as to how they might usefully engage in the science/religion debates and discussions they are likely to encounter at college.

Cyril Domb holds that science and religion are indeed opposed to each other—but only in the sense that the thumb is opposed to the fingers in order to secure a better grasp. He sees the two enterprises engaging in a new partnership.

It is clear that a proper sense of awe is integral to the religious quest. As **Mary Midgley** stresses, it is not as generally recognized that the scientific drive is similarly motivated. Both pursuits derive their power through the exercise of open-minded wonder, rather than the adoption of dogmatic attitudes. For this reason it should not prove difficult to establish constructive and harmonious dialogue between them.

Pauline Rudd takes up a similar theme. She holds that the irresistible lifelong search for answers to questions calls for the exercise of the same human qualities, regardless of the field of endeavor—qualities such as courage, vision, integrity, perseverance, respect for others, commitment, and humility.

Science originally grew out of a religious context. Many of the unspoken philosophical bases that underpin science derive from theistic considerations. Its early practitioners saw nature as the handiwork of Almighty God, and themselves as exercising stewardship over the Earth. **Mehdi Golshani** puts forward the view that, if the pursuit of science and the development of its applications are to lead to the promotion of human happiness and welfare, scientists need to regain a theistic perspective on their work.

What I Want My Teenager to Know about the God/Science Debate

KITTY FERGUSON

My youngest child has left for university, and a phrase from the hymn-book keeps running through my head: "Classrooms and labs, loud boiling test-tubes, sing to the Lord a new song!" Will my daughter have ears for that music? Is she ready for serious challenges to her childhood faith in God?

I can't tell her that she must go on believing in God regardless; she will decide that for herself. But I have given her some guidelines.

Contrary to popular legend, university science faculties aren't all hotbeds of atheism. Certainly you will encounter scientific atheists, but many scientists believe in God and many others are agnostics. Why do the atheistic scientists believe there is no God? The answer is likely to be deeply personal rather than anything to do with science. If they do say science is the root reason, this is sometimes because they grew up with a narrow, impoverished picture of God—one that simply had to give way when science offered a richer view of reality. But some admit that even if the scientific evidence seemed to show there is a God, they probably wouldn't change their minds.

Science is not the atheistic superweapon that earlier generations thought it was. It doesn't rule out belief—even orthodox belief. Nevertheless, diehards continue brandishing the old weapon, often attacking some caricature of religion that science (and believers themselves) rule out. They may do this so noisily, and with such sarcasm and scorn, that it's hard to remember the gun isn't loaded.

But there is a more thoughtful argument. Rather than declare, "We can't believe this anymore in the modern age," it says instead, "We don't *need* to believe this anymore." This is an argument for agnosticism rather than atheism. The physicists Stephen Hawking and Jim Hartle, and the biologist Richard Dawkins, for example, try to show that there are possible explanations for the origin of the universe and for the emergence of human life which do not require a Creator. If your main reason for believing in God is that you think this universe couldn't exist if there wasn't one, then this kind of science could seriously undermine that belief. I hope your faith is based on more than God being a necessary explanation. The two questions "Is God *needed* as an explanation?" and "*Is* God the explanation?" are quite different.

Not that science has found an explanation for the way the universe appears to be incredibly fine-tuned to produce life. This fine-tuning is taken by some to be evidence of a Creative Purpose at work. They may be right. But will you rest your case there? Don't. Making science your primary way of deciding religious questions is like walking on shifting sands. Science considers the "unexplainable"—and indeed its own previous "knowledge"—fair game; both are overturned regularly. Always remember: God reportedly has said, "Seek me," not "Seek evidence of me."

If you argue for belief in God in a scientific-intellectual discussion, don't be surprised if you lose. Few undergraduates have the knowledge and expertise—or the experience living with the presence of God—to hold their own in such a debate. Don't worry. Whether there is a God and what God is like are not matters decided by any debate or argument, regardless of how well informed and deeply thought out. Either there is a God, or there isn't. God is like what God is like. Your eloquence or ineptitude won't make one jot of difference to the answer. You can rack up debating points and still be dead wrong; you can be demolished and still be right.

Science teaches you to live with unanswered questions and contradictions, sometimes to hold in mind two "truths" that, on the face of it, can't both be true. Putting a seeming contradiction "on hold" isn't doublethink when you do it knowingly. This is as true in religion as it is in science. It's a sign of maturity and high intellectual capacity.

Science builds on earlier knowledge. There have been great minds whose vision you should trust at least until you're sure of your own. Religion has people like that, too; they have wrestled with the same questions that disturb you. If you are prepared to trust Einstein until you're able to understand relativity for yourself, why not trust great spiritual leaders?

Science calls for a childlike approach. So does religion. Childlike means putting no limits on the "possible," being full of wonder, questioning what others take for granted.

It's right for you to strive for mature intellectual sophistication. But you should know that the great thirteenth-century philosopher Thomas Aquinas spent a lifetime in intellectual pursuits, arguing powerfully for the existence of God; he would have won the debate you lost. But later he had an experience of the presence of God, compared with which all that earlier endeavor seemed to him "like mere straw." People still have that experience in this age of modern science.

Seek out such people—deeply intelligent, educated, well-informed people who believe in God. Spend time with them. Barrage them with questions. They aren't easily deceived or self-deluded. They aren't naive; they may even be somewhat skeptical by nature. But they know what they know.

•

Kitty Ferguson studied at the Juilliard School. After a career as a professional musician, she became a full-time science writer. Among her books are the best-seller Stephen Hawking: Quest for a Theory of Everything *and* The Fire in the Equations: Science, Religion, and the Search for God.

God or Science: Do I Have to Choose?

 MARTINEZ HEWLETT

"Do I have to choose between God and science?" This question is asked by many students who come to college to study modern science, but who bring with them a religious faith based on what they learned in childhood.

The answer I give them is, "Of course not!" Why does that answer seem so unusual and perhaps even glib? It is because in our culture the encounter between science and religion is painted by extremists. Students are constantly, and in unsubtle ways, being told in class by a number of their professors that, at best, religion is distinct from science, or at the extreme, belief in God and the investigation of the natural world cannot coexist.

Some of these teachers hold that science and its empirical method can and will eventually answer any and all questions that the human mind can pose. This new belief system, called "scientism," is based on the assumption that the scientific method is the "only way" of gaining any understanding of reality.

Thus, belief in God and adherence to a religious view, though possibly beneficial, are treated as meaningless human behaviors—the view expressed by E. O. Wilson in his book *Consilience*. Richard Dawkins is of the opinion that theism is an unacceptable position to be held by any intelligent and educated person. The idea that one must choose between science and religion is reinforced when one hears fundamentalist voices from the religious community declaring that science is, indeed, "Godless."

What is actually going on here? Are these two deeply human enterprises truly at odds? The answer becomes clear when one recognizes that scientism is a misunderstanding of the goal of investigation of the physical world, as practiced by everyone from Galileo to Charles Darwin to

178

James Watson and Francis Crick. Science is only one of many possible ways of viewing the world as it exists. The self-imposed limitations of the methods of science restrict the kinds of knowledge that can be gained by them.

At the same time, those who look to sacred Scripture for a literal description of the workings of the natural world, in their attempt to fend off the prevailing secular and materialist tide engulfing Western culture, have missed the real purpose of these precious writings. This was made clear centuries ago when Galileo, in his letter to the Grand Duchess Christina, quoted the words of Cardinal Baronius that ring true for us today. We need to reflect on the idea that "the intention of the Holy Spirit is to teach us how one goes to heaven, not how heaven goes."

I argue that a realistic understanding of both science and theology reveals areas of rich contact and even of possible confirmation, to use the categories described by the Georgetown University theologian John Haught. A critical and realistic view of science and religion reveals that they each have their separate domains and methods. And yet there are also points of distinct contact and communication.

Science asks questions of the physical world that can be answered by elegant instrumental measurements. These yield the clues and insights to be used in building our picture of the material universe. But the "what?" and "how?" queries often lead the investigator to the inevitable "why?" question. It is here that we find the scientist has no tools to address this kind of question. This is the sphere of the philosopher and of the theologian.

Too often scientists, lacking any training in theology, are tempted to extend their results far beyond their own area of expertise and venture to draw conclusions about religious issues. This is akin to a philosopher or theologian walking into one of our molecular biology classes and, with no training in the sciences beyond the high school level, attempting to interpret data and critique the theoretical models being used.

Theologians and philosophers, meanwhile, must be wary of entering into scientific discussions untrained and unprepared. For them to contribute meaningfully to the interdisiplinary discussions, they must operate with a clear understanding of the current models that science has constructed to explain how the physical world functions. Admittedly, such models of nature are tentative and always subject to revision. Nevertheless, philosophical and theological reflection and comment should take place within the worldview held by the current culture.

It is only from within this framework that issues of ultimate meaning and ethics can be approached. Any attempt to answer the question "Why are we here?" must be preceded by a reasonable idea of how we got here and what *here* actually is.

So, what do I say to my students? They enter the classroom on the first day of their freshman year, eager to begin the long journey toward a degree in one of the biological sciences and perhaps a career in medicine, research, or teaching. As they sit in that hall, with its tiered array of desks and walls adorned with the periodic table of the elements, I ask them to take a realistic view of the science in which they are about to be immersed for at least four years. I challenge them to think critically about the methods they will employ, the models they will build, and most important, the limitations of both.

Can God be present at the same time that they take their first steps on this path? Yes. Since there is only one reality and that reality is the work of the Creator, operating through the natural laws that we attempt to fathom, then, by definition, God is already there.

Martinez Hewlett is Associate Professor in the Department of Molecular and Cellular Biology at the University of Arizona. He is coordinator of the Forum on Theology and the Sciences at the Catholic Newman Center and a lay member of the Order of Preachers (Dominicans). His first novel was Divine Blood.

Science and Religion: Heading for Partnership?

CYRIL DOMB

Science and religion, sworn enemies in the past, seem to be heading for partnership in the twenty-first century. Look at the titles of some of the books published in the last decade: *Can Scientists Believe?* by Nevill Mott, *The Mind of God* by Paul Davies, *The Science of God* by Gerald Schroeder. These are not the works of eccentrics but leading academics.

There have always been scientists who were also deeply religious— Isaac Newton, Michael Faraday, and James Clerk Maxwell are outstanding examples. But these represented a small minority, and until recently most of their colleagues were agnostics. In the latter half of this century, however, avowed secularists have started to put God into their thinking.

Fred Hoyle, a distinguished astrophysicist and cosmologist, is a typical example. Hoyle started his scientific career as an atheist. After World War II, while puzzling about the proportions of the different elements, hydrogen, oxygen, carbon, iron, lead, and so on, in the universe—why some are common, and others rare—he had a bright idea. Suppose that they were formed in the vast hot interiors of stars in the early development of the universe; it should be possible to calculate the proportions of the elements present in the universe today from the structure of nuclei revealed by laboratory experiments of nuclear physics. Hoyle started on this program and soon encountered a serious obstacle. Carbon is essential to life, but with the data at his disposal it would be unstable and would not survive. The only way out was a daring idea that there existed a hitherto undiscovered energy level in the tiny carbon nucleus. Experiments were set up, and the level was found exactly as predicted. Hoyle became convinced that this was not a coincidence but evidence of intricate design.

During the following decades, evidence of design came to light elsewhere. The masses of two basic constituents of matter, the electron and the proton, were already known at the beginning of this century. Their ratio is a "constant of nature." No one paid much attention to it. But then scientists became aware that its precise value was of vital importance—if it changed even by a minute amount, life as we know it would no longer be possible. Not only that, the same kind of "fine-tuning" was found in other constants of nature and in basic aspects of the astronomy of the universe.

Conclusions have therefore been drawn in accord with religious thinking. First, that there is design in the universe—as Hoyle puts it in his autobiography: "The atheistic view that the universe just happens to be here without purpose and yet with exquisite logical structure appears to me to be obtuse." Second, that human beings are an important feature in the design of the universe—to quote Freeman Dyson, a top theoretical physicist, "I do not feel like an alien in the universe. The more I examine the universe and study the details of its architecture, the more evidence I find that the universe in some sense must have known that we were coming." This contrasts markedly with the conventional evolutionary view that we humans emerged unplanned.

The advantage of forging links between science and religion becomes evident not only in trying to understand the universe at large and how we living creatures come to be here, but also closer to home. I refer to the way science and technology are impacting upon society.

We are all conscious of the benefits that are conferred by this type of research and development. Every aspect of our daily life has been affected. Houses are comfortable in all weathers, the standard of living has improved greatly, automation has removed the drudgery from menial jobs and shortened the working week. Modern transport enables us to travel with ease, advances in medicine have greatly increased the expectation of life, and the explosion of information has enabled us to obtain precise knowledge on any subject of interest.

But we have also become aware of certain undesirable consequences when science and technology are given a free hand. Waterways have become polluted by chemical waste, the use of nuclear reactors has given rise to terrifying accidents like Chernobyl with serious long-term effects, and the discharge of certain gases into the atmosphere may be leading to global warming with unforeseeable consequences. The discovery of insecticides seemed at first to be a gift from heaven to protect and increase our food supplies. But after a few years the original insects were killed off, and their place was taken by more virulent and resistant strains. Birds and chickens which ate the insects became poisoned; the insecticides found their way into human bodies and caused cancer. Rainfall washed the chemicals into the Earth and into water supplies.

The discovery of the structure of the molecule DNA which controls genetics and inheritance in living creatures has opened the door to genetic engineering. Now, it would seem, the genes which control personality, ability, and other traits handed down by parents to their children might be changed. How wonderful if hereditary defects which cause hemophilia, sickle-cell anemia, cystic fibrosis, and other dreaded diseases could be corrected. But how alarming if the power to change human personality were exploited. This has recently hit the headlines when scientists succeeded in cloning a sheep. Might this be extended to human beings? A host of questions is arising which science on its own is not equipped to tackle. Why not take religion as a partner?

Albert Einstein, the greatest scientist of this century, wrote in 1942: "Religion without science is blind, science without religion is lame." Some twenty years earlier another great scientist, William Bragg, had said the following: "Sometimes people ask if religion and science are not opposed to one another. They are; in the sense that the thumb and fingers of my hand are opposed to one other. It is an opposition by means of which anything can be grasped." It is significant that when the British government recently established a committee to report on the ethics of cloning, they chose as chairman John Polkinghorne, a distinguished high-energy physicist, who moved to theology and became an ordained priest. Perhaps this is a herald of the twenty-first century.

●

Cyril Domb, F.R.S., is Emeritus Professor of Physics at Bar-Ilan University in Israel; he was formerly academic president of the Jerusalem College of Technology and Professor of Theoretical Physics at King's College, London. Domb was awarded the Max Born Prize in 1981.

The Need for Wonder

MARY MIDGLEY

Are science and religion at war? The idea that these two concerns ought to fight each other arose about a century back. Today, plenty of scientists believe that the notion is due for a rethink.

A hundred years ago, religious and scientific sages did indeed engage in some fierce power struggles. The churches were then strong forces in society, especially in the control of education. Scientists wanted to wrest that control from them, and also to get properly paid for their own work. So it is not surprising that battles followed. In the upshot, the scientists gained in status and the churches lost a good deal of their power.

Of course, some such battles do still continue today. But on the whole that power struggle is now a thing of the past. And in any case, these are social matters. What about science and religion themselves? Are they really opposite forces?

In answer to this we cannot help but note a striking similarity in the motives out of which these two concerns flow: both are rooted in a sense of wonder.

Clearly, this is true of religion. Whether it recognizes one God or many, whether it reveres nature itself or the forces for good that we find in it, religion always flows from a sense of awe at something that is greater than ourselves. But what of the pursuit of science?

Most people readily accept that scientists are motivated by curiosity—the desire to understand the world and how it operates. But note, this is not mere idle curiosity. It is not indiscriminate, not just a casual yen for collecting facts. It is not satisfied by gossip or by qualifying for Mastermind.

What is not generally appreciated is that serious scientists experience a sense of awe. They are usually drawn to ask questions about a particular thing in the natural world. It may be flowers or stars, or it may be something that other people do not care for at all—toads, beetles, tape-worms. Whatever it might be, the study of this thing moves them to reverence. And make no mistake, this sense of reverence is real. Scientists can sense the vastness of even the smallest things. They know that these things have unending connections with the rest of life.

For that reason, their experience of wonder does not vanish when the questions have been answered. To a real scientist, a question that has been answered becomes not less wonderful but more so. Increased understanding increases scientific awe. And most great scientists have named awe of this kind as their deepest reason for pursuing science at all.

That is why these scientists are never, in the crude sense, "reductive." They are not trying to expose the things they inquire about as frauds. They are not keen to say things like, "When you get right down to it, a human being is nothing but ten dollars' worth of chemicals." They may indeed be trying to find out just what those chemicals are. But they know this is not a terminus. They know there is no "nothing but" about it. They know that each thing they discover about the chemicals only shows them more questions. Always, however long they might go on, there will be more things that they don't know about the ways in which those chemicals are put together.

Are these scientists, then, dispelling the mysteries of the world? Are they losing wonder? Of course, they do dispel particular mysteries, but wonder survives. For instance, we know now that the continents move. That is no longer a mystery. But *how* do they move? The river of questions that springs up about this is endless. And even where particular questions do get answered, the mere fact that continents *can* move remains incurably a subject for astonishment and awe.

187

What, then, have the scientists done here? They have not just discovered some new facts. (Facts can be trivial—even new ones.) And they have not just been showing off their puzzle-solving skill by putting the facts together in new ways. What they have done is to increase our understanding. They have changed our imaginative vision of the world. They have shown us how to look at the facts differently so that the picture makes more sense. This is a kind of work which always involves wonder. It calls for a sense of the vastness of things. It cannot be done by the kind of intelligence that is merely the power to solve problems.

That kind of intelligence is mechanical. It cannot find new problems or decide which problems are the most urgent. It has to go on down its street, doing what is called "normal science." It is what is measured in intelligence tests. But that is not what we mean when, in common speech, we say that somebody is *intelligent*. If we say this, we mean that they have a fresh, imaginative way of looking at the world. They can see beyond the puzzles that are put on their plate. They try to look honestly at the vast world from which those puzzles are drawn. So they know how much they do not know.

And obviously, this same kind of open-minded intelligence is also needed in religion. People who think they have doctrines that settle the vast questions raised by religion have not started to grasp what they are trying to do. In the past, dogmatic attitudes of this kind have, of course, often set off feuds between religion and science. We ought to know by now that, on both sides, they are always mistaken.

●

Mary Midgley was formerly Senior Lecturer in Philosophy at the University of Newcastle. Her books include Beast and Man, Evolution as a Religion, Science and Salvation, *and* Utopias, Dolphins and Computers.

Science and Religion: What Is It All For?

PAULINE RUDD

What is the meaning of our existence? What, if anything, is the point of all our efforts to live for more than mere physical survival? Why are our dreams of a world founded on beauty, truth, and peace so compelling? And why do we ask so many questions and drive ourselves to meet impossible challenges?

Many, if not all of us, have encountered an irresistible urge to commit ourselves to a lifelong search for answers to questions such as these. Moreover, in the moment of commitment we have felt the adrenaline flow and our pulses race as our hearts beat faster. Instinctively, we recognize that we are not choosing an easy option, that the journey will involve incalculable risk, that the search will require "blood, toil, tears and sweat," and that the best we have to offer of ourselves will be scarcely sufficient for the task.

In the beginning, we do not even know exactly what it is that we are seeking. Like the knights of King Arthur in search of the Holy Grail, we have to enter the forest at the darkest place where there is no path.

We are not in competition with one another; the quest will take each of us along a different way. Although we learn constantly from those around us, in the end we are responsible for faithfully following our own paths, for it is only by so doing that each of us will make our unique contribution to the sum total of human knowledge and insight.

The qualities which have long been recognized as essential in such a quest include courage, vision, integrity, perseverance, respect for others, commitment, humility, and that all-encompassing, multifaceted attribute, love. These are words laden with poetic overtones. But they are also the everyday ideals which we have come to expect everyone to live up to, whether they are company directors, scientists, artists, theologians, explorers, artisans, nurses, or politicians.

The knights of King Arthur, as well as great religious thinkers and philosophers, knew that unless we aspire to such virtues, none of us can hope to reach our full potential. As St. Paul implied in his letter to the Corinthians, we may acquire faith enough to move mountains and we may come to understand all mysteries, but if we are without love, all our labor, all our effort, and all our pain are worth precisely nothing.

Our shared experiences bind us together and far outweigh our differences. Whatever our calling, all our searches for meaning are conceived in the mists where the unknown beckons us with all its potential and infinite possibility. We all struggle to express our fleeting, dreamlike understanding of reality.

For some, those first contemplations are transformed into the posing of a question or a series of experiments; others express them in music or sculpting; and yet more of us interpret them as an encounter with the living God. Our need to come to terms with our creative gifts commits us all to the search for articulate expression through which we can share our experience with others. We persevere at every level to find the precise note, the true color, the exact word, the definitive experiment.

Moreover, the conversion of our dreams to reality exposes us all to the possibility of failure, of disclosing our inadequacy, of corrupting what appeared pure and incorruptible before our attempts to grasp, define, and give form to that which we experienced in the mist. Small wonder that the moment of commitment to the quest is sometimes terrifying, is always awe-inspiring, invariably requires courage, and needs to be accompanied by a vision of what could be achieved.

Further, to enrich and develop our own contribution it is essential for us to share our experiences with those whose paths are different from our own. For the scientist and the religious person to engage in a discussion in which there is a meeting of minds is no trivial task. Courage, vision, integrity, perseverance, respect for others, commitment, humility, and love are never more needed than when we contemplate sharing something infinitely precious to us with someone whom we believe may not appreciate it or, worse still, may despise it.

Our generation is engaged in the large-scale compartmentalization of knowledge. Ours is an age of specialists, and information overload is a daily reality. It is safer to stay with the systems we know best, where we have authority and insight. However, the fundamental question "What is all our increased knowledge for?" needs addressing urgently, and by us all. We have to dare to talk to one another, even to risk having to change our ideas in the light of new information. If we are to understand even a little of the essence of the universe, the nature of God, or what it means to be a human being, we need to combine all the insights we can derive from our various perspectives.

Science has opened up undreamed-of vistas in fields such as communication, space exploration, genetic engineering, robotics, and medicine. The great religions of the world are a priceless heritage which, uniquely, have the potential to integrate and express every aspect of human experience through poetry, art, music, symbol, and ritual. They can evolve to accommodate the deepest hopes and aspirations of each new generation. But for this to happen we all need to reflect on the current knowledge emerging from our particular discipline and to relate this to the innermost needs of the human spirit.

•

Pauline Rudd is University Lecturer and Senior Research Fellow with the Glycobiology Institute at the University of Oxford. She is an Associate of the Anglican community of St. Mary the Virgin, Wantage.

Theistic Science

MEHDI GOLSHANI

Why hasn't the progress of science brought joy and real happiness to humankind?

No one can doubt the great advances in scientific knowledge since Sir Isaac Newton's era: progress in communications, the supply of human material needs, and the control of diseases. However, to offset these, we also witness in the industrialized world many disturbing developments: a marked rise in suicide, a feeling of nihilism, drug abuse, depression, stress, and conflicts between nations.

In my view, much of the trouble lies in the philosophical bases underpinning modern science. Originally, science arose in a religious context. Its pioneers saw nature as the handiwork of an All-knowing Almighty God. They also saw humankind's role to be the stewardship of the Earth. But over the past two centuries this picture changed. Science in its modern form is silent about God and about our responsibilities toward ourselves, society, and the world. The prevalent view now concentrates on exploring nature and putting it at the service of human beings.

This current outlook misses two important facts. First, our world is much richer than empirical science appears to show. Second, to secure our welfare, there has to be a sense of responsibility in scientific work as in all human actions. We do not expect this responsible attitude to stem from science itself; it must be brought to science.

Science is usually thought to be an objective pursuit, being neither Eastern nor Western. Recent studies in the philosophy and sociology of science, however, have revealed that all theories of science are highly colored by philosophical biases or religious convictions.

Any scientific venture has two stages. One is the gathering of facts. The other is data grouping, concept making, and theory building. It is mainly in this second stage that philosophical or religious biases enter. This is what makes a science theistic or atheistic.

In order to understand what a theistic science entails, let me give a few examples.

First, consider the ability of science to make precise predictions. It is based on our trust in the lawfulness of nature. When we find a law that applies in certain cases, we believe that it will apply in all cases. But why do we assume that? Science itself cannot account for our trust in the intelligibility of nature or the reliability of scientific laws. Such trust, however, becomes natural in the context of a theistic science. This is a science based on a belief in a consistent personal God who created a planned cosmos which includes morally responsible human beings — a God who gave us the ability to grasp nature.

Second, consider the origin and development of the cosmos—the science of cosmology. Our knowledge of the universe is gained through the light received from outer space. This provides us with a few clues. But to go further and formulate a model of the cosmos, we have to make some assumptions. We assume, for example, that the laws of physics valid on Earth hold true at all times and in all places. We also assume that our position in the cosmos is not a favored one. These assumptions are not provable by the methods of empirical science. But they can be grasped on a theistic ground—the unity and harmony of the created world being a reflection of the unity of its Creator.

Finally, we consider the emergence of life in the cosmos. Recent studies have shown that life cannot emerge unless there is fine-tuning between the four basic forces of nature (gravitational, electrical, and two kinds of nuclear force). In fact, to have some of the elements necessary for life (e.g., carbon, nitrogen, oxygen, and phosphorus), they have to be made in the interiors of stars with proper conditions of temperature, density, and so on. The creation of these necessary conditions, in turn, depends sensitively on the initial state of the cosmos and the relative strengths of the basic forces. How are we to account for this fine balance between the four forces of nature?

The theistic account ascribes this fine-tuning of conditions to design—God deliberately designed the world to be a home for life. Scientists with an atheistic bias, on the other hand, assume there to be an infinite number of worlds, each having different strengths for the basic forces of nature. By chance, some of these worlds meet the needed conditions for the development of life.

So, the same set of observations, but two quite different interpretations of what lies beyond the common science. In one, it is assumed that there are infinite worlds; in the other, a supernatural God.

A scientist's worldview affects not only his or her choice of theories but also the direction which he or she gives to the applications of science. As we clearly witness, the uses of science in the recent past have not always been for our welfare. In fact, a large number of scientists are involved in the making of deadly weapons or things harmful to humanity or our environment. A theistic outlook urges scientists to use their knowledge in the service of promoting happiness and welfare.

●

Mehdi Golshani is Professor of Physics and Chairman of the Philosophy of Science Department at Sharif University of Technology in Tehran, Iran. Among his recent books are The Holy Qur'an and the Sciences of Nature *and* Can Science Dispense with Religion?